WHAT ARE WE HOPING FOR?

NEW TESTAMENT IMAGES

Daniel J. Harrington, s.j.

D0324686

LITURGICAL PRESS
Collegeville, Minnesota

www.litpress.org

Cover design by Monica Bokinskie

1	2	3	4	5	6	7	8

Library of Congress Cataloging-in-Publication Data

Harrington, Daniel J.
  What are we hoping for? : New Testament images / Daniel J.
  Harrington.
     p. cm.
  Sequel to: Why do we suffer?
  Includes bibliographical references.
  ISBN-13: 978-0-8146-3161-4 (alk. paper)
  ISBN-10: 0-8146-3161-4 (alk. paper)
  1. Hope—Biblical teaching. I. Title.
BS2545.H64H37   2006
225.6'4—dc22   2006000719

CONTENTS

Prologue: Hope and the Bible   v

Part I: Images of Hope in Matthew's Gospel   1

   1. Emmanuel   4

   2. Star   6

   3. Water   8

   4. Fishermen   11

   5. Salt and Light   14

   6. Father   16

   7. Boat   18

   8. Meals   21

   9. Yoke   23

   10. Kingdom   26

   11. Rock   28

   12. Vineyard   30

   13. Bridesmaids   32

   14. Cry   35

   15. Resurrection   37

Part II: Images of Hope in Paul's Letter to the Romans   41

   1. Gospel   44

   2. Salvation   46

   3. Sacrifice   49

    4. Abraham   51
    5. Justification   54
    6. Adam   56
    7. Death and Life   59
    8. The Divided Self   61
    9. Spirit   63
    10. Childbirth   65
    11. Remnant   67
    12. Olive Tree   70
    13. Body   72
    14. Night and Day   74
    15. House   77
Part III: Images of Hope in the Book of Revelation   80
    1. One Like a Son of Man   83
    2. Tree of Life   85
    3. Slain Lamb   87
    4. Four Horsemen   90
    5. White Robes   92
    6. Scroll   94
    7. Woman   97
    8. Beasts   99
    9. Seven Plagues   102
    10. Harlot and Bride   104
    11. Rider on a White Horse   106
    12. Millennium   108
    13. Last Judgment   110
    14. New Jerusalem   112
    15. River of Life   115
A Concluding Word of Hope   117
For Reference and Further Study   118
Index of Subjects   120
Index of Ancient Texts   121

Prologue

HOPE AND THE BIBLE

This volume is a sequel to my earlier book (2000) entitled *Why Do We Suffer? A Scriptural Approach to the Human Condition* (Sheed & Ward). In that work I took the experience of suffering, something we all know, as a key to reading large parts of the Old and New Testaments. In writing that book I was constantly aware that there is another, more positive side to biblical theology: hope. Indeed, the theme of hope flows naturally out of the problems and the texts treated in *Why Do We Suffer?*

The Bible is a book of hope, and it communicates its hopes largely through images or figurative language. I want to explore images of hope in three key New Testament books: Matthew's Gospel (a narrative about Jesus' birth and earthly career, and his Passion, death, and resurrection), Paul's letter to the Romans (a theological reflection on the significance of Jesus' life, death, and resurrection), and Revelation (a book of prophecy about the future and the present). I have chosen these three books because they are among the longest, most influential, and most difficult books in the New Testament. I will explore fifteen images of hope in each book. The audience for this book is not so much biblical specialists as members of the general public who may be interested in biblical studies and Christian theology. I will try to combine the positive and constructive results of modern biblical scholarship with the needs and interests of people today, who live in a world where hope often seems in short supply.

THE NATURE OF HOPE

Hope does seem to be in short supply these days. The images of airplanes crashing into the Twin Towers in New York City and the Pentagon in Washington on September 11, 2001, haunt the minds of most Americans and others all over the world. The plans and hopes of many people were dashed that day by a fiendishly brilliant team of terrorists. Likewise, the terrible scenes of material devastation and personal hopelessness associated with Hurricane Katrina and the flooding of New Orleans in late August of 2005 have been seared in the memories of us all. Of course, other peoples have their own personal and communal images that seem to cut off hope and make their efforts at planning seem a bad joke.

The hopelessness that seems to infect many of us today is ironic, since never have human beings been more able to control their environment and their future than they are today. The advent of new medicines has rescued many of us from much pain and suffering and increased our life expectancy dramatically. The perfection of heating and air-cooling systems in our homes and businesses has enabled us to live and work with greater efficiency than ever before. The mobility we have with all our modern modes of transportation—automobiles, airplanes, and high-speed trains—allows us to go halfway around the world in a matter of hours rather than days or years. We now have reasonable hopes of defeating diseases like cancer and HIV/AIDS in the near future. And how can I begin to list the benefits that computer technology has brought into our lives?

If hope seems to be in short supply today, this is due in part to our becoming victims of our own human progress. Now more than ever we face the prospect of an old age marred by Alzheimer's and Parkinson's diseases. To get the energy we need to control our environment, we use fuels that pollute our environment. The same airplane that may bring me safely home from a distant land may also bring a terrorist with an atomic device in his suitcase. And how much "SPAM" do you get daily in your emails?

Nevertheless, we all have hopes, we all know what hope is when we feel it, and yet we may not find it easy to define hope. Under their entries for "hope" the dictionaries include something like the following definition: Hope is a desire accompanied by the possibility of, or the belief in, its realization. That means that hope has an object or focus, looks toward the future, and has some basis or ground in reality. Without hope we would not get up in the morning. Indeed, throughout our lives most of us live from hope to hope.

The opposites of hope are presumption and despair. Presumptuous persons drift through life, assuming that they will be taken care of, or that God or someone else will do everything for them. Despairing persons are so overwhelmed by their own inadequacies and/or the obstacles before them that they often become emotionally inert. On the contrary, persons of hope have goals, recognize what they need to do to reach those goals, and try to shape their lives in accord with them. While the spectrum of presumption—hope—despair applies to all kinds of hopes, it is especially relevant when we take God to be the primary object of our hope.

The hope treated in this book is the theological virtue of hope. This is the hope we find all over the New Testament. It has God as its primary object, and in particular our right relationship with God and eternal life. It looks forward to the full coming of God's kingdom. And it has as its basis God's person and promises to his people, as well as the paschal mystery (the life, death, and resurrection of Jesus). This kind of hope may not transform natural pessimists into perpetual optimists. But it will guide us along the pilgrimage we call life, as we say and live out the words of the Lord's Prayer (Matt 6:9-13; Luke 11:2-4).

The hope promoted by the New Testament writers is founded on faith and expresses itself in love. Without faith there is no reason for hope. People of faith and hope want to share themselves and their vision with others and contribute to building a more just and humane society here on earth. They do so not only for the rewards they may expect in the present and the future, but also because they want to do good and follow the example of the God "who makes his sun rise on the evil and on the good" (Matt 5:45).

THE BIBLE AS A BOOK OF HOPE

The Bible as a whole is a book of hope. In the Old Testament hope is based on the person and promises of God, whether for offspring and land in the case of Abraham, for Israel's goodness and greatness as a people (Moses), for an ideal king like David (messianism), for Israel's return from exile (Isaiah 40–55), for the restoration of Israel as God's people under a new covenant (Jer 31:31-34), or for the vindication of the wise and righteous with the coming of God's kingdom (Daniel).

In ancient Greek thought the object of hope may have been life after death based on the immortality of the soul (Socrates, Plato) or happiness in this life (Aristotle). In New Testament times the object of hope for Jews took various forms: the renewal and restoration of Israel as God's people, the perfect observance of God's Law, the coming of the Messiah, the fullness of the kingdom of God and the vindication of the righteous, and so forth.

Among early Christians the basis for their hopes was the resurrection of Jesus and the gift of the Holy Spirit. Christian faith takes these two events as the past and present manifestations of the fullness that is still hoped for: eternal life with God, and the kingdom of God. Jesus' resurrection and the Holy Spirit in turn make it possible for Christians to live in confidence and patience in the present, since eternal life has already begun for them through faith and baptism, and that belief makes possible a positive and hopeful attitude toward God's future intervention.

IMAGES OF HOPE

In dealing with hope we all need images. By itself the word "hope" is often too abstract. We need to imagine the objects of our hopes, whatever they may be. Most of us learn best when we can associate principles and data with concrete images. In dealing with Christian hope in the New Testament it is even more necessary to rely on images. The principal hopes developed in the New Testament—right relationship with God, eternal life, and the kingdom of God—are beyond ordinary human experience. They involve the person and activity of God, and so are transcendental. Moreover, their fullness lies in the future, and often our only route to the future is the imagination. The transcendental and future hopes of Christians are best understood and expressed through images.

The main part of this book is a series of short essays on images of hope in Matthew, Romans, and Revelation, respectively. For each image there will be a title, a focal text, a brief reflection on the image itself, some (mainly Old Testament) background, a discussion of the image in the New Testament passage and book, and "reasons for hope" emerging from the presentation. There are also brief introductory discussions for each of the three biblical books.

Hope is an inexhaustible topic, and there are thousands of images of hope in the New Testament. I offer these brief essays as a sample of such images in three books. I also wish to illustrate a method of reading biblical texts that combines historical and literary analysis with theological reflection. I intend this book as a work of biblical theology. It is largely objective and descriptive. I want the biblical texts to speak for themselves. But I also write as a Catholic Christian, and so I do not altogether avoid the "we" language that expresses my solidarity with both the biblical writers and Christians today.

One tried and true way of reading and praying over biblical texts is *lectio divina* ("spiritual reading"). It consists of four steps: reading (what does the text say?), meditation (what does it say to me?), prayer (what do I want to say to God?), and action (what must I do?). These essays can help mainly with the step of reading the text carefully and intelligently, while the concluding remarks on "reasons for hope" may help readers with beginning their meditations. What readers might want to say to God or how they might shape their lives on the basis of these biblical images of hope is up to them and the Holy Spirit.

Part I

IMAGES OF HOPE
IN MATTHEW'S GOSPEL

Often described as the "most Jewish" of the four gospels, Matthew's narrative about Jesus is a book of hope. It presents Jesus as fulfilling many of the promises God made to his people Israel. Its traditional position as the first book of the New Testament makes it into a bridge between the two Testaments. Moreover, Matthew's gospel emphasizes that the fullness of God's kingdom remains in the future. It teaches us to pray: "Thy kingdom come!" (6:10). It ends with the promise of the risen Jesus to be "God with us" (Emmanuel) until that time. And by its extensive samples of Jesus' teachings it shows us how to live in the present as we await the full coming of God's reign.

As one of the four gospels in the New Testament, Matthew's gospel tells the story of Jesus' birth, his public activity as a Jewish teacher and healer, and his Passion, death, and resurrection. It has many features found in ancient biographies and puts Jesus forward as an example to be imitated. Nevertheless, it is also a document of faith in the sense that it was written from the perspective of belief in Jesus' resurrection and his identity as the Son of God. Its claims about Jesus transcend

1

what was said about ordinary mortals, and thus it presents
Jesus as the reason for extraordinary hopes.

The evangelist seems to have been a Jewish-Christian
teacher. He wrote for a community made up largely of Jewish
followers of Jesus. The early manuscripts (from the 4th and
early 5th centuries) contain the title "According to Matthew,"
thus reflecting the traditional ascription to Matthew the tax
collector whom Jesus called to be his disciple (9:9). The gospel
was composed in a place where Greek was spoken, with a large
Jewish population and a largely Jewish Christian community.
A likely setting is Antioch in Syria, though other cities in the
eastern Mediterranean would also fit the profile. The date of its
composition is generally placed between 85 and 90 C.E.

Matthew's gospel is a revised and expanded version of
Mark's gospel. It contains many more examples of Jesus' teachings that Matthew drew from a collection of Jesus' sayings des-
ignated by modern scholars with the letter Q and from other
traditional sources. It also seeks to give a Jewish Christian response to the crisis facing all Jews after 70 C.E.

In putting down the Jewish revolt that began in 66, the
Roman army captured Jerusalem and destroyed the Temple
there. This meant that the spiritual center of Judaism was no
more, and foreigners had even greater control over the Holy
Land. Matthew's response to this crisis was to claim that the
legacy of Israel as God's people was best carried on in the community formed around Jesus of Nazareth. He contended that
many of God's promises to Israel were fulfilled in Jesus, and
that adherence to Jesus' person and teaching was the best way
to prepare for the coming reign of God. Matthew's gospel is
about the hopes of God's people that had already been fulfilled
and about those yet to be fulfilled. Many scholars point to Matt
13:52 as a good description of the evangelist himself: "Therefore every scribe who has been trained for the kingdom of
heaven is like the master of a household who brings out of his
treasure what is new and what is old."

Because of the strong words against the scribes and Pharisees in chapter 23 and the negative portrayal of the chief priests and elders of the people in the Passion narrative, Matthew's gospel (the "most Jewish") is sometimes accused of being "anti-Jewish." But both Matthew and most of the people for whom he wrote were Jews and regarded themselves as Jews who found what they were looking for in Jesus the Jew. This gospel emphasizes the Jewishness of Jesus and God's fidelity to his promises made manifest in Jesus. However, Matthew's gospel (see 27:25) can be used for anti-Jewish purposes when taken out of its original historical context in the struggle within Judaism about who best carried on the heritage of Israel. Christians today need to respect that historical context and be sensitive to the gospel's anti-Jewish potential when taken out of that context.

Matthew's gospel begins with an Infancy Narrative (1–2) and ends with a Passion-Resurrection Narrative (26–28). The most striking structural feature is the five great speeches of Jesus: the Sermon on the Mount (5–7), the Missionary Discourse (10), the Parables (13), the Community Discourse (18), and the Eschatological Discourse (24–25). The chapters between the five speeches consist mainly of narratives about Jesus as a powerful healer and a wise teacher.

Matthew presents Jesus as the Son of God (having a relationship of special intimacy with God), as the Messiah (the one who incarnates and fulfills Israel's hopes), and as the Son of Man (the one who suffers and dies, and who will return in glory). The focus of Jesus' life and teaching is the kingdom of God (or heaven) that is both present in Jesus' person and future in its fullness. As "Emmanuel" Jesus is the presence of God among us and the basis of hope for the fullness of God's kingdom. Those who follow Jesus, while having "little faith," nevertheless take Jesus as their teacher, try to do what he does (teach and heal), and find in him the fulfillment of God's promises to his people and the ground of their hope for the future.

1. EMMANUEL (MATTHEW 1:1-25)

"'Look, the virgin shall conceive and bear a son, and they shall name him 'Emmanuel,' which means 'God is with us.'" (Matt 1:23)

Every child is (or should be) a sign of hope. That a virgin woman should conceive and bear a child is not especially unusual. But that such a woman should remain a virgin because this conception is through the Holy Spirit is very, very unusual. And that her child should be the presence of God among us (which is the meaning of the two Hebrew words that make up "Emmanuel") is even more remarkable. This is no ordinary child. As Emmanuel, this child is the basis of Christian hope.

Background: The text quoted in Matt 1:23 is Isa 7:14. The setting for that prophecy is the court of King Ahaz of Judah (735–715 B.C.E.). In that situation Isaiah of Jerusalem prophesied that a young woman (*ʿalmah*) in Ahaz's household (presumably the king's wife) would soon become pregnant, and that her son would grow up to be a good and righteous ruler (probably his son Hezekiah, who reigned from 715 to 687 B.C.E.). Indeed, so good and righteous would this child be that he would be celebrated as the presence of God ("Emmanuel") among the people of Judah.

Matthew: For Matthew, this prophecy of Isaiah (and many other OT passages) is fulfilled in the person of Jesus. But the word "fulfilled" does not adequately express Matthew's real perspective. To Matthew these prophecies were more than simply fulfilled in Jesus. Rather, they were fulfilled in a superabundant way.

In quoting Isa 7:14 Matthew followed the Greek translation of Isa 7:14, which renders the Hebrew term *ʿalmah* ("young woman") as *parthenos*. While the Greek word *parthenos* can mean "young woman," for Matthew it seems to have carried the more specific meaning "virgin." This is clear from the angel's words to Joseph: "the child conceived in her is from the Holy Spirit" (1:20; see 1:18). Moreover, since Matthew (and other early Christians) regarded Jesus as the Son of God, the evangelist believed that in Jesus the prophetic promise of "Emmanuel" ("God is with us") was fulfilled in Jesus far more dramatically and definitively than either Isaiah or King Hezekiah ever imagined. In the virginal conception of Jesus and in his role as "Emmanuel" the prophecy contained in Isa 7:14 was fulfilled in a superabundant manner.

According to Matthew the birth of Jesus stands both in continuity and in discontinuity with the great figures and events of ancient Israel's history. The genealogy (1:1-17) that introduces Matthew's account of Jesus' birth (1:18-25) is very orderly. It repeats many times the verb translated "was the father of" ("begat" in earlier translations). There are three series of fourteen generations each, and each series marks a decisive period in ancient Israel's history: from Abraham to King David (1:2-6a), from David to the Babylonian exile (1:6b-11), and from the Babylonian exile to Jesus' birth (1:12-16).

The sense of continuity and order is interrupted by the inclusion of four women, all of somewhat dubious reputation: Tamar (Genesis 38), Rahab (Joshua 2), Ruth, and Bathsheba the wife of Uriah (2 Samuel 11–12). In each case there is something odd or unusual about these women, thus contributing to the sense of discontinuity regarding the birth of Jesus and marking it as something very new and special.

Accepting the virginal conception of Jesus was not much easier for people in antiquity than it is for people today. According to Matt 1:19, Joseph suspected his fiancée Mary of adultery and contemplated divorcing her; see Deut 22:23-27 for an even harsher penalty. According to Luke 1:34, Mary's own initial response was doubt and confusion: "How can this be, since I am a virgin?" Their acceptance of the unusual and indeed impossible conditions surrounding the birth of Jesus was a sign of their hope and trust in God's word for them.

Reasons for Hope: Jesus was no ordinary child. From his conception onward Jesus is Emmanuel ("God is with us"). That was so not simply in the sense that God is on our side but rather that God has been, is now, and ever will be present among us. Throughout his public ministry Jesus shows himself to be a wise teacher and a powerful healer, leading people to ever greater wisdom and wholeness. He enters into the events of the Passion with the conviction that he undergoes suffering and death "for us" and "according to the Scriptures." And Matthew's gospel ends much as it began, with the promise of the risen Jesus that he will always be with us: "And remember, I am with you always, to the end of the age" (28:20). The first and last reason for Christian hope, according to Matthew, is the promise that through Jesus God is with us ("Emmanuel") in a superabundant manner, in a way the OT prophets could only glimpse, dimly hope for, and barely articulate.

2. STAR (MATTHEW 2:1-12)

> *"Where is the child who has been born king of the Jews?*
> *For we observed his star at its rising, and have come to pay*
> *him homage."* (Matt 2:2)

Stars have always fascinated humans. They appear as bright and shining lights against the dark sky. Their brilliance evokes admiration and hope from us. They bear witness to the order of the universe and provide perspective when life on earth seems chaotic and dangerous. They help soldiers and sailors to determine their direction and find their way on long journeys.

Background: In antiquity people thought that unusual astral phenomena marked the birth and death of famous persons. Scientists have long argued whether the astral phenomena that accompanied the birth of Jesus were due to a comet, or the birth of a new star (a supernova), or the conjunction of the planets Jupiter and Saturn. We can leave those arguments to the astronomers.

The biblical text most pertinent to the star as a sign of hope appears in Num 24:17: "a star shall come out of Jacob, and a scepter shall rise out of Israel." This statement is part of a prophecy by Balaam, a pagan prophet hired by Balak the king of Moab to prophesy against Israel. Try as he might, Balaam could only prophesy on behalf of Israel. Indeed, in Num 24:17 Balaam goes on to prophesy that the "star" will crush the Moabites and their neighbors. This prophecy was probably associated originally with David's victories over the Moabites and Edomites (2 Samuel 8), and was eventually applied to the Messiah hoped for by the Israelites.

Matthew: According to Matt 2:2, "Magi" from the east observed a star in the sky and connected it with the birth of "the King of the Jews," which was their way of referring to the Messiah of Israel. Moreover, according to Matt 2:9 the star directed the Magi to the exact place in Bethlehem where the King of the Jews was born.

The Magi have been identified as Persian priests and/or astronomers/astrologers from Babylon. The gifts they bring— gold, frankincense, and myrrh—suggest an association with Arabia or the Syrian Desert (see Ps 72:10-11). Whatever their origin, we are to assume that these visitors had studied the movements of the stars and believed that they could learn from them the mysteries of the present and future. In this sense they combined astronomy and astrology, and made a connection between the star and the Messiah of Jewish hope.

We are also to assume that the Magi were not Jews. The word "Magi," which originally referred to a caste of Persian priests, identifies them as foreigners in Israel. Moreover, they have to consult Jewish scripture experts to learn where the Messiah is to be born. In this context the Gentile astronomers/astrologers set out because of a strange star and their hope of finding the Messiah of Israel.

The Gentile Magi came to Israel to "pay homage" to the Messiah (2:2, 11). Their hopeful attitude contrasts with that of Herod the Great, the ruler in Israel from 37 to 4 B.C.E. The last thing Herod wanted was that the Magi or anyone else should find the Messiah, since if the Messiah is the real king of the Jews there would be no kingship for Herod or his sons. Whereas non-Jews seek out Jesus the King of the Jews in order to pay him homage, the officially reigning king of the Jews (Herod) wants to kill him off as a potential rival.

The star points out the presence of Jesus as the King of the Jews. By searching him out and paying him homage, the Magi foreshadow the command of the risen Jesus at the very end of Matthew's gospel: "Go therefore and make disciples of all nations" (28:19). Whereas at Jesus' birth the Gentile Magi come to him, at his resurrection he sends out his Jewish disciples to the Gentiles.

Reasons for Hope: The star was a sign of hope for the Magi. Whether out of scientific curiosity or for some other reason, they set out on their long journey in the hope of finding someone brilliant and important. For them the star in the heavens was a witness to the star/Messiah foretold by the pagan prophet Balaam. Their finding the king of the Jews indicates that the good news (gospel) of Jesus is meant for all the peoples of the world. Through Jesus the King of the Jews, people from all over the world can and do become part of the people of God.

3. WATER (MATTHEW 3:13-17)

"Then Jesus came from Galilee to John at the Jordan,
to be baptized by him." (Matt 3:13)

Water is one of the most common elements on earth. We need water to live. But we can also die from too much water, as in a flood or by drowning. Water therefore functions as a natural symbol that can signify life or death. The waters of the Jordan River run from north to south on the eastern side of the land of Israel. In those waters John the Baptizer exercised his ministry of immersion. There John baptized Jesus in water.

Background: John's rite of baptism had precedents in Jewish water rituals connected with the Jerusalem Temple. Priests were expected to wash before offering sacrifices (Exod 40:12). On the Day of Atonement the high priest was directed to wash before and after the sacrifices (Lev 16:4, 24). The Jewish religious group that lived at Qumran and gave us the Dead Sea scrolls constructed an intricate system of water channels that enabled them to observe their daily ritual purifications in accord with their priestly spirituality. In rabbinic times converts to Judaism underwent proselyte baptism as a sign of their accepting the Jewish way of life.

Although it had precedents in Judaism, John's baptism was different. While he used water and evoked the symbolism of cleansing and purification, John focused his baptism on preparation for the coming reign of God. His baptism was to be received only once, and it involved spiritual and moral conversion.

Matthew: According to Matt 3:2, John proclaimed: "Repent, for the kingdom of heaven has come near." These same words reappear in the summary of Jesus' preaching in Matt 4:17. John and Jesus say the same thing. However, Matthew also insists that John is subordinate to Jesus. In their fulfillment of Isa 40:3, John is the voice of the one crying in the wilderness while Jesus is the Lord whose way John prepares (Matt 3:3).

In Matt 3:11 there are contrasts between the persons and the baptisms of John and Jesus. John admits that Jesus is more powerful and that he is not worthy to carry Jesus' sandals (the task of a slave or servant). And John describes his own baptism as "with water for repentance," whereas Jesus' baptism will be "with the Holy Spirit and fire"—for both salvation and judgment. Even though John may well have served as Jesus' mentor, he recognized the superiority of Jesus.

That Jesus underwent John's water baptism is one of the most solidly established facts about Jesus' life. However, the description of John's baptism as being "for repentance" could cause a theological problem. Matthew 3:13-15 solves the problem

by appealing to Jesus' desires to fulfill God's will ("all righteousness") and to identify fully with his fellow humans.

Both John and Jesus were prophets of God's kingdom, and
so signs of hope. How powerful and extraordinary a sign of
hope Jesus was becomes clear in the events following his baptism by John. The conclusion of that ritual is marked by three
signs: the opening of the heavens, the Holy Spirit descending
"like a dove," and the voice from the heavens.

The three signs point to the breaking down of the barriers
between God and humankind in the person of Jesus. The opening of the heavens (see Ezek 1:1) indicates the possibility of di-
rect communication between God and humans through Jesus.
The description of the Holy Spirit's descent as "like a dove"
echoes the creation account in Gen 1:2 where the "spirit" of
God hovers over the waters. And the heavenly voice identifies
more exactly who Jesus is. All three signs contribute to a renewed sense of hope at the beginning of Jesus' public activity.

What the voice says about Jesus in Matt 3:17 combines
phrases from various Old Testament texts to identify Jesus as
the personification of biblical hopes. He is "my Son" (an allusion to the Davidic king as God's son; see Ps 2:7), "the Beloved"
(an allusion to Isaac in Gen 22:2), and "with whom I am well
pleased" (an allusion to the Servant of the Lord; see Isa 42:1;
44:2). Thus at the start of his public activity Jesus is identified
as the fulfillment of Israel's hopes for the Son of David, the Son
of Abraham, and the Servant of God.

Reasons for Hope: The ultimate biblical hope is the full
coming of God's kingdom: "Thy kingdom come!" (Matt 6:10).
The baptism of Jesus by John in the waters of the Jordan singles
out Jesus as the unique instrument by which God's people can
share in the presence of God's kingdom and prepare for its future fullness. In that sense baptism is the sacrament of sharing
in the life of God's Son and of living in hope of the full manifestation of God's reign.

4. FISHERMEN (MATTHEW 4:18-22)

> *"And he [Jesus] said to them, 'Follow me,*
> *and I will make you fish for people.'"* (Matt 4:19)

Fishermen live by their wits and practical skills. They engage in a necessary and sometimes dangerous profession. All over the world and for many centuries commercial fishing has been a major business venture. The first four disciples Jesus called to follow him (Matt 4:18-22) were commercial fishermen. They were two sets of brothers: first Peter and Andrew, and then James and John (Zebedee's sons). They were engaged in their family businesses when Jesus met them in the midst of their work on the shore at Capernaum. Fishing in the Sea of Galilee was a major business enterprise, and the first disciples owned the boats and nets necessary to engage in this kind of work. We should not take too literally the comment of their opponents in Acts 4:13 that Peter and John were "uneducated and ordinary men." It is unlikely that these commercial fishermen were totally illiterate.

In calling his first disciples Jesus alludes to their occupation as fishermen and urges them to use their wits and skills in "fishing" for human beings, in the sense of helping them to understand and appreciate Jesus' own preaching of God's reign.

Background: Jeremiah is often pictured as the prophet of doom and gloom. It is true that many of Jeremiah's prophecies are calls for Israelites to repent from their evil ways and threats about what will happen if they do not. We even have the English word "jeremiad" to refer to a prolonged lamentation, complaint, or harangue. However, there are oracles of hope throughout the book of Jeremiah. The most famous is God's promise of a "new covenant" with Israel and Judah (Jer 31:31-34).

Another prophecy of hope appears in Jer 16:14-18, where the prophet looks to a new gathering of Israel's exiles and a return to their land. This event, Jeremiah claims, will surpass in importance ancient Israel's exodus from Egypt. In describing how this dramatic gathering will take place, Jeremiah refers to some of God's agents as "fishermen": "I am now sending for many fishermen, says the Lord, and they will catch them" (16:16). The fishermen thus serve as signs of hope for a purified and renewed people of God.

Matthew: One of the puzzles in Matthew's account (4:18-22; also Mark 1:16-20) of Jesus' call of the first disciples is this: Why did Peter and Andrew, James and John follow Jesus so readily? According to the narrative these four fishermen had no prior knowledge of Jesus. While they were at work one day, Jesus came along and said: "Follow me," and they did. They had nets and boats, and so answering Jesus' call involved giving up their businesses. They had families, and so answering Jesus' call involved leaving their homes and forming a new family. Why did they answer Jesus' call?

The usual answer to this question appeals to the literary skill of the evangelists or their source. The utter simplicity of the narrative—Jesus calls and the disciples respond immediately—serves to highlight the personal attractiveness of the figure of Jesus. How persuasive and attractive Jesus must have been to inspire such an immediate and total response! There is much to be said for this interpretation, and it is not wrong.

But there may be more to it than that, especially when we read Matthew's account in its literary context and in the context of our theme of hope. I suggest that the first disciples followed Jesus out of hope—a hope rooted in the past, a hope that looked toward the future, and a hope that was based in the present.

First, the past: Matthew prefaces the beginning of Jesus' public ministry with a quotation in 4:15-16 from Isa 9:2: "The people who walked in darkness have seen a great light." That prophecy was uttered some seven hundred years before the birth of Jesus. It expressed the hopes of a people caught between their more powerful political neighbors and hoping for some kind of solution to their plight. Isaiah's prophecy also described well Israel's political situation in Jesus' time. For Jesus' contemporaries like the four fishermen and for early Christians like Matthew, Jesus was a light shining in the darkness. They saw Isaiah's hope being realized before their eyes in Jesus.

Second, the future: Immediately before the call of the first disciples Matthew places a summary of Jesus' preaching: "Repent, for the kingdom of heaven has come near" (4:17). "The kingdom of heaven" refers to God's establishing his rule over all creation. This is what we pray for when we say: "Hallowed be thy name; thy kingdom come; thy will be done on earth as it is in heaven." The central theme of Jesus' preaching was the coming reign of God. The first disciples hoped to be part of it. They hoped to experience that reign.

Third, the present: In 4:23-25 Matthew follows the call of the first disciples with a summary of Jesus' activities: teaching, preaching, and healing. As Matthew (and the other gospels) present these activities, they are ways in which Jesus makes manifest the presence of the reign of God among us. Jesus showed us how to live in the hope of experiencing the fullness of God's reign. The hope of the first disciples was based on the life and actions of Jesus of Nazareth as the prophet of God's reign.

Reasons for Hope: Why then did the four fishermen follow Jesus and become his first disciples? Surely they found him persuasive and attractive. But Matthew suggests that perhaps an even more basic reason was their hope. The fishermen hoped that Jesus would be the light shining in the darkness, in accord with Isaiah's prophecy. The fishermen hoped that Jesus' proclamation of the coming reign of God would come to pass. And the fishermen based their hope on Jesus' activities as a wise teacher, a trustworthy prophet, and a powerful healer.

5. SALT AND LIGHT (MATTHEW 5:13-16)

"You are the salt of the earth . . . . You are the light of the world."
(Matt 5:13, 14)

Salt and light are familiar to us all. We use salt to bring out the flavor in food and make it taste better. In antiquity, but also today in many parts of the world, salt is employed as a preservative to keep meat, fish, and other foods from spoiling. Thanks to modern electricity, light is all around us. But for most of human history light has been in short supply and so was even more precious and appreciated. Without light there is always great physical danger because we do not know what may be around us. Without light there is no sense of direction but only aimless wandering and terror.

Background: In biblical times salt was used as flavoring for food and as a preservative (Job 6:6). It was also associated with the sacrifices offered in the Jerusalem Temple and with the covenant (Lev 2:13; Ezek 43:24). God's first words in the Bible are "Let there be light" (Gen 1:3). Isaiah the prophet challenges the house of Jacob to "walk in the light of the Lord" (2:5). And Ps 43:3 calls upon God : "O send out your light and your truth; let them lead me."

Matthew: The images of salt and light are directed to the audience of the Sermon on the Mount (Matthew 5–7). Those who take seriously and put into practice the teachings of Jesus contained in the sermon are important and necessary for the welfare of the world precisely because they are people of hope.

These two images occur immediately after the beatitudes (5:3-12). The point is that those who live by the values of the beatitudes will be the salt of the earth and the light of the world. Each beatitude consists of two parts. The first part declares some persons or behaviors "blessed" or "happy," while the second part explains what rewards they can hope for.

The first part of each beatitude describes the personal qualities, characteristics, or behaviors of the true followers of

Jesus. They are poor in spirit, compassionate, meek, passionate about justice, merciful, people of integrity, peacemakers, and willing to suffer for justice and for the name of Jesus. These are the people who will enter God's kingdom and enjoy its fullness. These are the ways in which people of hope act. This is how dreams and wishes can be turned into realities.

What can those who live according to the beatitudes hope for? According to the second part of each beatitude, they can hope for the kingdom of heaven, comfort and consolation, a share in God's reign over creation, happiness, mercy from God, and being children of God. All these individual hopes are different aspects of the same great hope: fullness of life in God's kingdom.

According to Christian faith, what Jesus' life, death, and resurrection have made possible is right relationship with God (justification), eternal life with God, and participation in the kingdom of God when it comes in its fullness. From the beatitudes we learn about the ultimate goal or object of Christian hope, and what sort of people we must try to be and what we must do if we want to reach that goal and have our greatest hopes come to pass.

The remainder of Matthew 5 presents Jesus' teachings on various topics treated in the Old Testament Law: murder, adultery, divorce, oaths, retaliation, and treatment of enemies. Without abolishing these laws, Jesus puts them in a new key by challenging his followers to go to the root of the biblical commandments. If you want to avoid murder, avoid the anger that is at the root of murder. If you wish to avoid adultery, avoid the lust that is at the root of adultery. And so on. In this sense Jesus' teachings are radical, since they go to the "root" (Latin *radix*) of things. In this sense Jesus does not abolish the biblical commandments, but he does bring them to a deeper and fuller level.

Reasons for Hope: Those who live by Jesus' challenging teachings are the salt of the earth and the light of the world. As people of hope, they seek to turn their hopes into realities. They hope for the fullness of God's reign, and they find in Jesus' teachings the guidance and inspiration they need. Just as our lives are better for the presence of salt, people of Christian hope make the world a better place because of the goals they have and the values they espouse. Likewise, people of Christian hope bring light to what often seems like a dark world, give it joy and purpose, and provide positive guidance and direction. The vocation of the Christian is to be salt of the earth and light of the world. Only persons of hope can be that.

6. FATHER (MATTHEW 6:9-13)

"Our Father in heaven, hallowed be your name." (Matt 6:9)

In our world today family structures are changing rapidly. The ideal of the so-called nuclear family—two parents and several children—was not and is not always the case in practice. What has not changed is every child's need for an adult or adults to provide for them and protect them. Without some such guidance children run the risk of leading aimless and hopeless lives. Children need responsible parents.

Background: Ancient Near Eastern societies like biblical Israel were patriarchal in their social structures. The father or patriarch was the key figure insofar as he served as the provider and protector for his wife (or wives), children, and servants or slaves. He oversaw the activities of the members of his household, including their religious duties. He was expected to raise his sons strictly so that they might learn the meaning of patriarchal fatherhood, and he was responsible for arranging the marriages of his daughters. The wife and children in turn were expected to show honor and respect to the patriarch, at least in public settings. In this social framework all the members of the household were expected to bring their needs and requests to the patriarch, who would judge their value and do what he could to turn their hopes into realities.

Matthew: The one text in Matthew's gospel that every Christian knows is the Lord's Prayer (6:9-13). There is another, shorter, and perhaps earlier version in Luke 11:2-4. But Matthew's version is the one we all learn and use in private and public Christian prayer. The Lord's Prayer or "Our Father" is the prayer Jesus taught his disciples to use. It is the quintessential prayer of Christian hope, for in it we bring our greatest needs and hopes to God as our provider and protector.

The Matthean version of the Lord's Prayer is part of the Sermon on the Mount. It appears in the midst of three instructions about important Jewish (and Christian) practices of piety: almsgiving (6:2-4), prayer (6:5-15), and fasting (6:16-18). The fundamental challenge of these instructions concerns the motives we bring to doing them. Is it to gain a good reputation in society? Or is it simply to serve God? Jesus insists that if these acts of piety are to be genuine, they must be undertaken only out of respect and love for God. The Lord's Prayer sits right at the center of these instructions

One of the best established facts about Jesus is his relationship of special intimacy with God expressed in his use of the word "Father." While not without precedent in Judaism, Jesus' use of "Father" as a name for God was surely characteristic of his understanding of and approach to God. And he invited his followers to approach God as Father in the same way, with the appropriate honor and respect, in the hope that our heavenly Father might grant us what we need most.

The body of the Lord's Prayer in Matt 6:9-13 consists of three "you" petitions and three "we" petitions. All of them concern the full coming of God's kingdom, which is the goal and horizon of all genuine Christian hope.

In the "you" petitions we ask God as Father to grant three great hopes. The first is that God's name may be "hallowed" by all creation. That means that all creation might acknowledge the sovereignty of God and join in the angelic chorus of praise found in Isa 6:3: "Holy, holy, holy is the Lord of hosts; the whole earth is full of your glory." The second hope, which is really a restatement of the first, is that God's kingdom might come in its full glory. While there are anticipations of God's reign in the present and while Jesus in his life and ministry was himself the presence of God's kingdom, there always remains the hope for an even greater display of God's reign in the future. The third hope, which is really a restatement of the first two, is that God's will may be done on earth as it is in heaven. Here we ask for an end to evil and sin among us, and for the salvation of our world.

The three "we" petitions ask God for help as the fullness of God's reign draws near. We first ask God to sustain and support us physically, and to give us a taste of the bread of life here and now. Then we beg for forgiveness from God and promise in return to forgive others who may have given us offense. Finally we pray for protection and deliverance in the midst of the testing that will accompany the definitive manifestation of God's kingdom and for support in the midst of life's trials.

Reasons for Hope: The Lord's Prayer is the preeminent prayer of Christian hope. It is the prayer for the fullness of God's reign. That is what we hope for, and it seems to have been the central theme of Jesus' own activity and preaching. It is addressed to God as "our Father in heaven." The address expresses our beliefs in the transcendence of God ("in heaven") and the immanence of God ("Father"), and reminds us that we always make this prayer as a community ("our") of hope for the coming reign of God.

7. BOAT (MATTHEW 8:18-27)

> *"A windstorm arose on the sea,*
> *so great that the boat was being swamped by the waves."*
> (Matt 8:24)

Fishing in any body of water can be dangerous, especially when the boat is small and fierce storms come up suddenly. Much of Jesus' early ministry took place near the Sea of Galilee, a large body of fresh water, eight miles broad at its widest point, and thirty-two miles around, in northern Galilee. His first disciples were fishermen. Some years ago, due to a severe local drought, a two-thousand-year-old fishing boat was discovered by the shore of the Sea of Galilee. While larger than a small rowboat, it was clearly too small to ride out a severe storm with ease.

Background: For ancient Near Eastern people, especially those who lived near the Mediterranean coast, the sea was often a symbol of uncontrolled power or chaos. Some imagined creation as God imposing order or control over the wild forces of the sea (Genesis 1). Psalm 107:23-30 provides a striking picture of the terrors associated with a storm at sea: "They [the sailors] mounted up to heaven, they went down to the depths; they reeled and staggered like drunkards, and were at their wits' end" (107:26-27). The only hope for sailors in such chaos was prayer: "Then they cried to the LORD in their trouble" (107:28a).

Matthew: The Sermon on the Mount in Matthew 5–7 has shown Jesus to be powerful in word. There he appears as a wise and challenging teacher. Matthew 8–9 shows Jesus to be powerful also in action, especially as a healer, an exorcist, and one able to harness the forces of nature and overcome death. Jesus first heals a leper, a centurion's paralyzed servant, and Peter's mother-in-law (8:1-17). Then he manifests his power over a storm, demons, and sickness and sin (8:23–9:8). Finally he heals two women, two blind men, and a mute man (9:18-34). These acts of divine power are interrupted by challenges to discipleship (8:18-22; 9:9-17), and serve to introduce Jesus' lengthy missionary discourse (9:35–10:42).

One of the most interesting episodes in this collection of miracle stories is the account of Jesus stilling the storm at sea (Matt 8:23-27). An earlier version appears in Mark 4:35-41. There after a day spent in telling parables about God's reign (Mark 4:1-34), Jesus suggests that he and his disciples go across to the eastern shore of the Sea of Galilee. The fishermen take him in their boat. But when a sudden storm arises they find themselves in danger of drowning. Meanwhile Jesus is asleep in the stern of the boat. When in their panic they awaken Jesus, he commands the sea: "Peace! Be still!" The wind stops, and immediately all is calm. Then Jesus upbraids the disciples for their lack of faith. They in turn ask, "Who then is this, that even the wind and the sea obey him?" (4:41).

The answer to the disciples' question can be found in Ps 107:29: "he [the LORD] made the storm be still, and the waves of the sea were hushed." With that fundamental insight Matthew in 8:18-27 rewrote Mark 4:35-41 to bring out more sharply certain themes present in his source.

According to Matt 8:18, Jesus gives an order (not a suggestion) to go over to the other side. Meanwhile when approached by two prospective disciples (8:19-22), Jesus reminds them that his disciples face the prospect of homelessness and must put following him before all other (even sacred) obligations. Resuming the story, Matthew has the fishermen follow Jesus into the boat (8:23). The storm is so great (8:24) that Matthew describes it as a *seismos* (the Greek word for earthquake). The disciples awaken Jesus (8:25) not with a rebuke ("do you not care?") but with a prayer ("Lord, save us! We are perishing!"). Jesus answers by asking: "Why are you afraid, you of little faith?" (8:26). When Jesus rebukes the winds and sea, there is "a dead calm." The disciples are amazed and ask in 8:27: "What sort of man is this, that even the winds and the sea obey him?" We already know the answer from Ps 107:29.

There is a longstanding debate whether for Matthew (and Mark) the boat was a symbol of the church. There is no doubt, however, that very early in Christian history the boat became such a symbol. Even today it is customary to refer to the church as "the bark of Peter." The boat symbolism alludes to the occupation of the first followers of Jesus, and underlines the threats facing the church and its fragility when regarded as a merely human institution.

Reasons for Hope: Taking the boat as a symbol for the church, we are made aware of both the dangers to the church and its intrinsic weakness in the face of them. Nevertheless, in all ages the church's hope has resided not in itself but rather in the Lord who remains with it as "Emmanuel." Recognizing its own "little faith," the church needs to pray as it tries to navigate through the chaotic storms around it and within it. In every generation the church's prayer should be the words of the frightened Galilean fishermen: "Lord, save us! We are perishing!" This is a prayer of genuine Christian hope.

8. MEALS (MATTHEW 9:9-13)

"And as he sat at dinner in the house, many tax collectors and sinners came and were sitting with him and his disciples." (Matt 9:10)

Meals are natural occasions in every human culture. Most of us like to share conversation and fellowship as we eat and drink. We mark special occasions with opportunities to share a meal. From these meals together we hope for deeper personal relationships and greater wisdom. From ancient times until today, a special gathering for sharing wisdom has been called a "symposium," which derives from the Greek word for "drinking together." The image of the meal has several levels.

Background: In biblical times it was customary to ratify agreements or covenants with meals held in common. Most sacrifices offered at the Jerusalem Temple involved meals with family and friends. In the wisdom books the figure of Wisdom invites all who seek wisdom to a grand banquet at her house (see Prov 9:1-6). When Jews of Jesus' time imagined what life would be like when God's kingdom came in its fullness they often employed the image of the banquet. And they sometimes pictured the Messiah as presiding at this banquet. Their meals were images of hope for the coming reign of God.

Matthew: One of the most striking and controversial features of Jesus' public ministry was his custom of sharing meals with marginal or disreputable people. This practice was scandalous to many of his religious contemporaries. Both Pharisees and Essenes conducted fellowship meals with religious overtones. However, their meals were controlled and exclusive; only the "right" people could come.

We are told that Jesus welcomed "tax collectors" and "sinners" to his meals. The tax or toll collectors like Matthew were suspected of stealing from the proceeds and collaborating with the Roman occupiers of the Holy Land. The sinners were people who displayed immoral behaviors or engaged in occupations that did not allow them to observe all the precepts of the Jewish Law. Both groups were not the kind of people with whom a Jewish religious teacher like Jesus was expected to share meals.

Nevertheless, according to Matt 9:9, Jesus calls a tax collector named Matthew to follow him and become his disciple. And Matthew the tax collector immediately gets up and follows Jesus. Then presumably at Matthew's house (9:10) Jesus shares a meal with many tax collectors and sinners. In doing so Jesus was presenting an "enacted parable" about God's reign and his own ministry. Like the Old Testament prophets Jesus performs an action as a way of teaching about God's reign. He was showing that some very surprising persons can and will be part of God's kingdom, and that only those who recognize their unworthiness and need for God's kingdom can hope to enter it.

The Pharisees did not understand Jesus' enacted parable. Their own exclusive fellowship meals were central to their lifestyle and piety. Why would Jesus of Nazareth, who had much in common with them, eat with such marginal and disreputable people?

In response to the Pharisees' complaint, Jesus gives two answers. One sounds like a proverb: "Those who are well have no need of a physician, but those who are sick do" (9:12). Healthy persons do not need doctors; sick people do. Thus Jesus presents himself as offering spiritual healing to marginal and disreputable people. The second answer is a quotation from Hos 6:6: "I desire mercy, not sacrifice." Here Jesus presents himself as the agent of God's mercy. Instead of condemning marginal and disreputable persons he offers them the opportunity to turn to God and enjoy the fullness of God's reign.

From Matthew's perspective Jesus was the Messiah, and his meals were anticipations of the messianic banquet that will mark the full coming of God's reign. The point of Jesus' enacted parable of sharing meals with tax collectors and sinners was to teach that the final messianic banquet will include surprising people and that there is always hope even for the most unlikely persons.

Reasons for Hope: Jesus had his greatest success not with the rich and famous but rather with the marginal and disreputable. His meals were signs of hope not only regarding God's reign but also the kinds of people who might hope to participate in the messianic banquet. People came to Jesus' meals in search of spiritual healing and divine mercy. When we come to the Eucharist, which is the sacrament of Christian hope, we too come in the hope of spiritual healing and divine mercy.

9. YOKE (MATTHEW 11:25-30)

"Take my yoke upon you, and learn from me." (Matt 11:29)

A yoke is an unlikely image of hope. The yoke was a device for harnessing animals—oxen, donkeys, cattle, and so on. It was placed on the neck and shoulders of the animals. The yoke made it possible for those beasts to work more effectively alone or in teams in plowing fields or powering mills.

Background: While the image of the yoke was often used to refer to situations of oppression or servitude, the prophet Jeremiah twice (Jer 2:20; 5:5) described his people's rebellion against God's law in terms on their breaking the yoke (which had previously kept them going in the right direction). The early second century B.C.E. Jewish wisdom teacher Jesus Ben Sira used the image of the yoke in an even more positive way. In Sir 6:24-31, Ben Sira urges those who seek wisdom to accept her yoke in the sense of hard work and discipline, and to regard wisdom's yoke as a "golden ornament." In 51:26-27 he invites prospective students at his wisdom school in Jerusalem to put their necks under wisdom's yoke and prepare to receive instruction and serenity. The rabbis spoke of observing the Jewish Law in terms on taking upon oneself "the yoke of the kingdom of heaven."

Matthew: The gospels present Jesus as a Jewish wisdom teacher. During his earthly ministry Jesus taught about topics routinely treated by other Jewish wisdom teachers: social relations, happiness, marriage and family, money, material goods, relating to God, and so on. And he used the literary forms typically employed by Jewish wisdom teachers: maxims, proverbs, instructions, prohibitions, admonitions, parables, questions, and beatitudes.

In Matt 11:28-30 Jesus of Nazareth sounds a lot like Jesus Ben Sira of Jerusalem. He invites prospective disciples to take his yoke upon themselves and promises them rest for their souls. He describes his own teachings as an easy yoke and a light burden. He claims that those who seek genuine wisdom will find it and more in his school. The wisdom of Jesus, however, transcends mere human wisdom because it comes from God.

The invitation to Jesus' school of wisdom is part of a larger passage (Matt 11:25-30) that appears in a context (11:1–12:50) that is mainly concerned with the unbelief and rejection Jesus received from many in Israel. Those who reject him have doubts about who he really is and whether his teachings can be trusted to come from God. Matthew 11:25-30 explains why Jesus' teachings should be accepted and why some people have rejected them.

In Matt 11:25-26 Jesus thanks his heavenly Father for revealing the divine mysteries to "infants" and hiding them from "the wise and the intelligent." In 11:27 he acknowledges that God's revelation is the source of his own wisdom and the origin of his identity as God's Son. His supreme wisdom comes from the Father, and as the Son he was sent to reveal this wisdom to humans. As the Son, Jesus is the revealer of the divine wisdom given to him by the Father. In 11:28-30 Jesus returns to the theme of the recipients of his revelation. He invites those who are weary and burdened to take his "yoke" upon themselves. Here the yoke image is not one of oppression or servitude. Rather it refers to the genuine freedom one can enjoy by studying under a teacher who is humble and gentle, one who promises and gives rest for the soul. The paradox is that the yoke of Jesus is easy and his burden is light. Thus Jesus transforms the yoke into an image of hope.

There are indications that Matthew's gospel was composed in the midst of a struggle among various Jewish groups about how best to preserve and carry on biblical Israel's identity as the people of God. With the capture of Jerusalem and destruction of its Temple by the Romans in 70 C.E., it was not at all clear that Israel would survive. Some Jews (the forerunners of the rabbis) focused their attention on perfect observance of the Torah, while others (apocalyptists) looked for a dramatic divine intervention and still others (Zealots) planned another political-military revolt.

In this historical context Matt 11:25-30 makes the early Christian case that Jesus as the Son of God is the wisest and best interpreter of the Jewish tradition. For those with open minds ("infants" before God) and seeking genuine "rest," Jesus' example and teachings were the best way to carry forward the Jewish heritage.

Reasons for Hope: There are many ways to wisdom, many sources of wisdom, and many teachers of wisdom. But Christians have a unique school of wisdom, one that features a gentle and humble teacher, imposes an easy yoke and a light burden, and promises rest and peace of soul. In the school of Jesus the yoke is an image not of oppression or servitude, but rather of hope.

10. Kingdom (Matthew 13:1-52)

*"The kingdom of heaven is like a mustard seed
that someone took and sowed in a field."* (Matt 13:31)

There are not many kings left in our world today. Nevertheless most of us can easily grasp the images of king and kingdom. Jews in Jesus' time certainly heard about the Roman emperor, but few ever saw him. They were more familiar with Herod the Great, who ruled the Holy Land as a kind of client king of the Roman emperor from 37 to 4 B.C.E. There was, however, an ancient tradition in Israel that understood God as the only real king.

Background: Many of the Psalms celebrate the kingship of God: "The Lord is king, he is robed in majesty" (Ps 95:1). Some scholars speculate that such psalms were composed to be part of the annual new year's festival in ancient Israel that focused on the kingship of God. However, with its successive subjugations after 587 B.C.E. to the Babylonians, Persians, Greeks, and Romans, there was a tendency in Israel (see especially the apocalyptic book of Daniel) to look forward to a dramatic manifestation of God's kingdom in the future.

Matthew: The kingdom (or reign) of God seems to have been the central theme of Jesus' teaching and healing activity. Matthew captured this emphasis with his initial summary of Jesus' preaching: "Repent, for the kingdom of heaven has come near" (4:17). Along with some other Jews of his time, Matthew wished to avoid using the word "God" too freely and out of respect substituted "heaven" for "God." What Jesus and the early Christians along with many of their fellow Jews hoped for was the full manifestation of God's reign. Their prayer was "Thy kingdom come!"

By its nature this kingdom belongs to God, and it is God's gift to give. Moreover, its fullness is future—so much so that its coming will mark the end of human history as we know it. The best and most effective way to think and talk about this kingdom is through images and analogies. That is why Jesus used parables to teach about the reign of God. The word "parable" refers to placing one thing beside another. A parable is a story taken from nature or everyday life about some interesting or surprising case that points beyond itself to another (spiritual) level. Matthew 13 contains several parables that begin with the formula "the kingdom of heaven is like . . . ." While the kingdom of heaven is the master image of Christian hope, it can be best understood with the help of other images of hope.

The short parables about the tiny mustard seed and the small amount of leaven (13:31-34) suggest that the small beginnings represented by Jesus' ministry will issue in the great conclusion that will mark the full coming of God's kingdom. The short parables about the buried treasure and the precious pearl (13:44-45) highlight the extraordinary importance of God's kingdom and the total commitment it deserves.

The longer parables about the wheat and weeds (13:24-30) and the dragnet (13:47-48) indicate that the full coming of God's reign will be accompanied by a divine judgment in which the good and the bad will be separated. The parable of the sower (13:3-9) warns that not everyone will accept Jesus' proclamation of God's kingdom, but promises that those who do accept it will bring forth spectacular results.

With such images Jesus sketches the present and future dimensions of his master image. Regarding the present he teaches that God's kingdom is present now in small ways, that for those with eyes to see it is the most important thing imaginable, and that we should live in active preparation for its full and final manifestation. With regard to the future he teaches that there will be a still more dramatic manifestation of God's royal rule, that its time and manner are God's prerogatives, and that it will involve a judgment that will separate the good from the bad.

Reasons for Hope: The full manifestation of God's reign is both the goal and the horizon of all Christian hope. Jesus taught us to pray for this: "Thy kingdom come!" As a wise and effective teacher Jesus used images, stories, parables, and all kinds of figurative speech to describe a reality that is ultimately transcendent and future, and so beyond our human comprehension. He elucidated the master image of God's reign with other images taken from the everyday lives of his original audience of farmers and fisherfolk in first-century Galilee: seeds growing, bread rising, finding buried treasure or a precious pearl, and fishing with nets. All are images of hope for God's kingdom. In doing this Jesus encouraged us to use our imaginations in thinking and talking about God and God's coming reign.

11. Rock (Matthew 16:13-20)

"You are Peter, and on this rock I will build my church."
(Matt 16:18)

A major insurance company (Prudential) takes as its symbol a huge rock, the Rock of Gibraltar. The logo conveys a sense of stability, strength, and permanence. It suggests that this company is going to be around for a long time, and those who deal with it can rely on the company and its promises. To say (as Matt 16:18 does) that the church is to be built on a rock means that it will be stable, strong, and permanent. The reason why is that it is founded on God's promises.

Background: The metaphor of "rock" is used with regard to God in 2 Sam 22:2-3 (see also Ps 18:2): "The Lord is my rock, my fortress, and my deliverer; my God, my rock, in whom I take refuge." Here God appears as a source of strength and a place of refuge. The idea of God as a rock of refuge occurs also in Ps 71:3. In Isa 32:2 the just rulers hoped for in the future are compared to "the shade of a great rock in a weary land." In these contexts the rock is someone or something that one can rely on for stability, strength, and permanence, and thus serves as an image of hope.

Matthew: The image of the rock appears most famously in Jesus' blessing of Simon Peter in Matt 16:18. That blessing (16:17-19) is part of the dialogue between Jesus and Simon Peter in 16:13-23, which is found also in Mark 8:27-33. When Jesus asks in 16:13, "Who do people say that the Son of Man is?" his disciples give various answers. But when he asks, "Who do you say that I am?" Simon Peter responds: "You are the Messiah, the Son of the living God" (16:16b). After declaring Simon Peter "blessed" or "happy," Jesus counsels silence about his true identity (16:20), prophesies his own death and resurrection (16:21), and rejects Peter's attempt to deny the necessity of his suffering and death (16:22-23).

The blessing of Simon Peter appears only in Matt 16:17-19. In it Jesus first in 16:17 praises Simon for recognizing his true identity ("You are the Messiah, the Son of the living God") and attributes this recognition to a divine revelation. Then in 16:18 he calls Simon by what seems to have been a nickname (*Petros,* meaning "Rocky") and promises to build his church on this "rock" (*petra*), which in turn will overcome all the forces of evil arrayed against it.

Some interpreters see the "rock" to be Peter's confession of faith in 16:16 or Jesus himself ("the church's one foundation"). But the most obvious referent is Simon Peter (*Petros*) as the "rock" (*petra*) on which Jesus will build his church. The text involves a pun on Peter's name and the word for "rock." While the word play works in Greek (*petros-petra*), it works even better in Aramaic (*kepha'* for both). The point is that the church built upon the rock of Peter will be a place of stability, strength, and refuge, and thus a source of hope. Then in 16:19 Jesus promises to give Peter the "keys of the kingdom of heaven" (see Isa 22:22) and the power to bind and loose (see Matt 18:18).

In many respects Simon Peter was an unlikely figure to receive such a promise. While Peter was one of the first disciples Jesus called, and served as the spokesman and leader for the twelve apostles, several gospel passages portray him as a somewhat impulsive and even unstable character. In Matt 14:28-31

Peter's attempt to join Jesus in walking on water results in his nearly drowning and being singled out as the exemplar of "little faith." In 16:22-23 Peter is rebuked as "Satan" for trying to dissuade Jesus from the way of the cross. And in 26:69-75 Peter denies Jesus three times and flees. While Matthew clearly revered Peter, he does not shrink from presenting his negative side.

What transformed Peter and made him into the "rock" on which Christ's church is built seems to have been his experience of the risen Jesus. That made Peter into a fearless preacher of the gospel who according to Christian tradition died as a martyr in Rome. Thus Peter is an image of hope on two counts: He is the exemplar of the forgiven sinner, and he is the rock on which Christ builds his church. Thus Peter is both a model of Christian hope and an object of hope.

Reasons for Hope: If God could make Simon Peter into the "rock" of stability and refuge, God can so transform anyone. The impulsive and wavering Simon Peter who showed "little faith" and denied even knowing Jesus became the rock on which the church of Christ is founded. This startling transformation reminds us that the ultimate source of Christian hope is the crucified and risen Jesus, and that therefore there is hope for us all.

12. VINEYARD (MATTHEW 21:33-46)

"There was a landowner who planted a vineyard, put a fence around it, dug a wine press in it, and built a watchtower." (Matt 21:33)

Most of Palestine in Jesus' time was an agrarian society; that is, the majority of people supported themselves by agriculture. While some had their own land and did subsistence farming, many farmed as sharecroppers the land of wealthy landowners and still others supported themselves through day labor on other people's property (see Matt 20:1-16). The landowners generally lived elsewhere and relied on tenant farmers to get the work done and pay the owner the largest share of the profits.

Background: In Isa 5:1-7 the vineyard is an image of Israel as the people of God: "the vineyard of the Lord of hosts is the house of Israel, and the people of Judah are his pleasant planting" (5:7). The vineyard that was expected to yield good grapes from which wine could be distilled yielded wild grapes instead (5:2a). This was despite all the care that God bestowed on his vineyard: "He dug it and cleared it of stones, and planted it with choice vines; he built a watchtower in the midst of it, and hewed out a wine vat in it" (5:2a-b). As a result God threatens to turn the vineyard into a "waste" (5:6).

Matthew: From the way in which the parable in Matt 21:33-46 begins, there is no doubt that it deliberately plays off Isa 5:1-7. The vineyard is clearly a symbol of Israel as the people of God. However, there is one big difference: Whereas in Isa 5:1-7 the problem is with the vineyard (Israel as a whole), in Matt 21:33-46 the problem is with the tenant farmers (the political and religious leaders of Israel).

Working from the earlier version of the parable in Mark 12:1-12, Matthew took over and developed its allegorical features in light of his own historical situation in the late first century. He means us to understand that the vineyard is Israel as the people of God, the landowner is God, the tenant farmers are the leaders in Israel, the slaves sent to collect the owner's profits are the prophets, the son is Jesus the Messiah, and the harvest is the coming reign of God and the last judgment.

Matthew's version of the parable places emphasis on the rejection of the prophets and the murder of Jesus the Son of God by Israel's bad leaders: "So they seized him, threw him out of the vineyard, and killed him" (21:39). It also seems to allude to what happened to Jerusalem and its Temple in 70 C.E., when the Roman armies came and put to death the Jewish leaders (see 21:41). And it suggests that God has taken the leadership of God's people away from the former leaders and given it to new leaders (the Jewish Christians).

According to Matt 21:41, the new leaders ("other tenants") will give to their master (God) the expected produce at harvest time (the reign of God). This point is made explicit to the chief priests and Pharisees in 21:43: "Therefore I tell you, the kingdom of God will be taken away from you and given to a people that produces the fruits of the kingdom."

The issue facing Matthew and indeed all Jews after 70 C.E. was: How can the heritage of Israel as God's people be carried on without the Jerusalem Temple and without political control of the land of Israel? Matthew's answer was that with the coming of Jesus the leadership of God's people has been transferred to those gathered around Jesus as their authoritative teacher and Lord: "you have one teacher, and you are all students" (23:8). Matthew wrote his gospel to explain what that statement means. He presents Jesus as the authoritative interpreter and fulfillment of the Jewish tradition.

Reasons for Hope: The image of the vineyard highlights God's continuing care for his beloved people. Note that the vineyard is not destroyed. Rather, the tenant farmers are replaced in order that the vineyard might be preserved and flourish. The vineyard (Israel) continues to be God's people, and God continues to care for it. A church without a historical and spiritual connection to Israel was unthinkable for both Jesus and Matthew. Their problem was not with Israel as God's chosen people but rather with the people's political and religious leadership. Matthew's parable of the vineyard teaches us to look forward in hope to the fullness of God's kingdom under the guidance of the risen Jesus as Emmanuel ("God is with us"), who promises to be with his people until the end of this age (28:20).

13. BRIDESMAIDS (MATTHEW 25:1-13)

"Ten bridesmaids took their lamps and went to meet the bridegroom. Five of them were foolish, and five were wise." (Matt 25:2-3)

A wedding is generally a sign of great hope. We have hopes for the couple bring married, for their many years of happiness and growth together, and for the children that their union may produce. They in turn are supported by the hopes their families and friends bring to the wedding. However, weddings are often complicated rituals involving many people, each with specific roles and functions. Much can go wrong. One traditional role at weddings is that of the bridesmaids. These women are expected to attend to and support the woman being married.

Background: In biblical times the high point of the wedding ceremony came with bringing the bride to the house of the groom or his family. Most of these weddings were arranged between the families of those to be married. There was usually a long period of engagement (as much as a year) in which the young people could get to know each other under supervision. When the groom (or his father) and the father of the bride determined, the wedding might take place. In Jesus' time this involved the signing of a written document with certain legal stipulations, including the "bride-price" for the father of the bride. When the document was signed and duly witnessed, the bride and groom made their way together in a kind of procession to his household, and their arrival was marked with a grand celebration.

Matthew: The bridesmaids in the parable presented in Matt 25:1-13 fit into the biblical marriage scenario. These young women (*parthenoi* in Greek, which can also mean "virgins") belong to the household of the groom. Their task is to receive the new bride into the groom's household. They are to attend to and support the bride during the reception and celebration.

According to the parable, the bridesmaids go out to meet the wedding party as it makes its way to the groom's household. The five "wise" or "prudent" bridesmaids take along a lamp or torch plus a supply of extra oil, while the five "foolish" ones merely bring their lamps. Since the groom is delayed, the bridesmaids become drowsy and go to sleep.

When the bridal party finally draws near at midnight, all the bridesmaids awaken and prepare to do their part in the wedding celebration. And so they light their lamps. The "foolish" bridesmaids soon run out of oil and ask the wise ones to give them some of their oil. The latter refuse on the grounds that they all will run out of oil before the wedding party arrives and there will be no bridesmaids to meet the wedding party.

While the foolish bridesmaids are off in town trying to buy some oil they miss the wedding party's arrival. The wise ones, however, can do their duty because they have brought extra oil, and so they accompany the bride to the groom's household, where the wedding banquet will take place. Meanwhile the foolish ones find themselves locked out of the celebration. The message of the story is: "Keep awake, therefore, for you know neither the day nor the hour" (25:13).

The wedding scenario in the parable of the ten bridesmaids would have been familiar enough to people in the time of Jesus and Matthew. But they, like us, may well have asked: What does this parable tell us about the reign of God? The answer is to be found in Matt 25:13. The full coming of God's kingdom is certain. But when it will come remains unknown: "You know neither the day nor the hour." The point is: Be vigilant always, stay awake always, be on guard always!

The parable of the ten bridesmaids is part of the eschatological discourse in Matthew 24–25. There Matthew takes over with some modifications to the discourse in Mark 13. But beginning with 24:37 Matthew adds a series of parables through 25:30 and climaxes his discourse with the judgment scene in 25:31-46.

The parables all serve to illustrate the need for constant vigilance stated in 25:13. The short parables about the days of Noah (24:37-39), the two men in the field and the two women at the mill (24:40-44), and the faithful and unfaithful servants (24:45-51) stress the uncertainty about the precise time of the kingdom's arrival and the importance of constant vigilance. The parable of the talents (a large sum of money in antiquity) in 25:14-30 stresses the value of imaginative and productive

activity in face of the judgment that will accompany the arrival
of God's reign in its fullness. The judgment scene in 25:31-46
with its image of the glorious Son of Man separating the sheep
and the goats specifies the criteria to be used in the last judgment: deeds of lovingkindness to "the least of these my brothers and sisters" (25:40, 45).

Reasons for Hope: The ultimate object of hope for Christians is the fullness of the reign of God. It is God's work to bring
the kingdom, and its fullness is future. This hope demands patient waiting for God to act. But we "know neither the day nor
the hour." Our hopeful waiting, however, is not mere passivity.
Rather, it demands constant vigilance and imaginative and productive activity in the present. The coming of God's reign will
involve a definitive judgment. The best way to prepare for that
judgment is through good works. Christian hope is not wishful
thinking or daydreaming. Rather, it inspires and issues in appropriate action in the present.

14. CRY (MATTHEW 27:45-54)

*"And about three o'clock Jesus cried out with a loud voice . . .
'My God, my God, why have you forsaken me?'"* (Matt 27:46)

To suffer is to undergo or feel pain or loss. We can suffer at
different levels: physical, psychological, and spiritual. People
cope with suffering in many ways: flight, resistance, explana-
tion, or transforming it into a discipline or an opportunity. In
the midst of suffering we tend to feel isolated and alone, even
though we all recognize that suffering is a universal experience.
We invariably ask "Why?" even though often there is no easy
answer. And in the midst of suffering most of us try to find
some reason for hope.

Background: Many of the 150 psalms in the canonical book
of Psalms (3, 5, 6, 7, 13, 17, and so on) are classified as laments.
These laments are addressed directly to God. They include

complaints about the present suffering and requests for God to do something about it. They usually express trust or confidence that God will act, and often conclude with a thanksgiving because God has already acted or will surely do so in the future. Throughout the centuries the lament psalms have allowed suffering persons to get in touch with their intense emotions, to recognize that they are not alone in their suffering, and to ask the basic theological question "Why?"

Matthew: According to Matt 27:46 (and Mark 15:34) the last words of Jesus were the first words of Psalm 22, one of the biblical laments: "My God, my God, why have you forsaken me?" Taken by themselves and without context they sound like a cry of despair. People often ask: Did Jesus despair at the moment of his death? Did he lose hope?

Such a negative interpretation makes no sense in the context of Matthew's gospel or any other canonical gospel. Jesus is always the model of hope. In fact, in the context of Psalm 22 and Matthew's gospel, the last words of Jesus are words of hope. In order to understand the last words of Jesus we need to take account of the whole of Psalm 22.

The first part of Psalm 22 (vv. 1-21a) is addressed directly to God ("My God, my God"). It begins by alternating complaints (vv. 1-2, 6-8) and professions of trust in God (vv. 3-5, 9-11). Then it moves into a lengthy complaint cast in striking images (vv. 12-18), and issues in a petition for divine deliverance (vv. 19-21a). By making his own the words of Psalm 22, Jesus identified himself with suffering people in all ages. Part of becoming fully human ("the Word became flesh and dwelt among us," John 1:14) was sharing in our human suffering. Jesus underwent a very painful death. In antiquity crucifixion was regarded as an unusually cruel way to die. It was entirely appropriate that Jesus, who suffered greatly, should recite Ps 22:1-21a.

But in Psalm 22 and in the case of Jesus, suffering does not have the last word. That psalm, like most of the biblical laments, ends on a note of hope and vindication. The second part of Psalm 22 (vv. 21b-31) tells how the speaker had been rescued and vindicated by God: "From the horns of the wild oxen you have rescued me" (22:21b). The hope expressed in the lament section had been fulfilled. And in response he wants to thank God in a public manner. Indeed, he wants to offer a sacrifice and to invite his relatives and friends (and even the whole world) to join in the celebration. He wants everyone to know what God had done on his behalf and wants future generations to recognize that "he [God] has done it" (22:31). So when we read the whole of Psalm 22 we find that it is a psalm not of despair, but rather one of hope.

Reasons for Hope: According to Matthew (and Mark) Jesus died with the opening words of Psalm 22 on his lips. In doing so Jesus identified himself with all his brothers and sisters who have suffered and still hoped. The Word became flesh and dwelt among us. At the same time Psalm 22 describes the vindication of the suffering person. For Christians the resurrection was the vindication of Jesus. He hoped in his heavenly Father and his hope was justified. And the resurrection of Jesus has become the ground of Christian hope. Psalm 22 is both the lament of a suffering person and the song of one who trusts in God and hopes for vindication from God. Hope, not suffering, has the last word.

15. RESURRECTION (MATTHEW 28:1-20)

"He is not here; for he has been raised, as he said." (Matthew 28:6)

The Greek verb *(anistemi)* behind "resurrection" means "to rise up, get up, stand up." Resurrection in its theological sense involves the restoration to "bodily" life after death. It is not the same as resuscitation or immortality of the soul. Rather, it concerns the revival of the whole person. The resurrection of Jesus is the ground of Christian hope. It gives shape to Christian hope because it is an event of the past, present, and future.

Background: Resurrection is not a prominent theme in the early parts of the Hebrew Bible. But in the early 6th century B.C.E., Ezekiel 37 used the metaphor of resurrection in the valley of the "dry bones" to describe the prophet's hope that Israel in exile in Babylon might come to life again as a people. Written in the second century B.C.E., Dan 12:2-3 looks forward to the resurrection of the wise in terms of their being awakened from the sleep of death to enjoy everlasting life. In the dialogues between the wicked king Antiochus IV and the seven brothers and their mother in 2 Maccabees 7 there are frequent appeals to the resurrection of the body and to rewards and punishments after death. From first-century B.C.E. Alexandria, the book of Wisdom proclaims that "the souls of the righteous are in the hand of God, and no torment will ever touch them. . . . Their hope is full of immortality" (3:1, 4).

Matthew: In Jesus' time the Pharisees were the great proponents of belief in the resurrection of the dead. According to Matt 22:23-33, the Sadducees (who rejected belief in resurrection) seek to trip Jesus up by offering an extreme and even absurd case. A woman who had married seven brothers in turn and each had died—whose wife will she be in the resurrection of the dead? Jesus contends that the Sadducees understand neither the power of God nor the Scriptures. He ends up siding with the Pharisees against their antagonists, the Sadducees, about resurrection.

The belief of the early Christians in resurrection went beyond what Jews in Jesus' time held. They claimed that Jesus had been restored to life after his death on the cross. Most Jewish proponents of resurrection expected that it would be a collective event and part of the full coming of God's kingdom and a prelude to the last judgment. But early Christians maintained that Jesus had been restored to life before the end-time—or rather, they held that the resurrection of Jesus had already begun the sequence of end-time events that will issue in the full manifestation of God's reign.

There is no explicit description of the resurrection of Jesus in the New Testament. In Matthew's gospel (and other parts of the New Testament) the tradition about Jesus' resurrection takes the form of narratives about the empty tomb, appearances of the risen Jesus, and the commission to carry on what Jesus began.

The empty tomb account in Matt 28:1-8 does not in itself prove the resurrection of Jesus. But it does seem to be a necessary condition for the interpretation given in 28:6: "He is not here; for he has been raised, as he said." The phrase "as he said" alludes to the three "Passion predictions" (16:21; 17:22-23; and 20:17-19), which each contain a "resurrection prediction" as their climax and conclusion.

Matthew surrounded his empty tomb narrative with several supporting passages. In 27:57-61 Mary Magdalene and the other women see Jesus die, watch him be taken down from the cross, and observe where he is buried. Then in 27:62-66 Pontius Pilate allows the Jewish officials to place a guard over and seal the tomb of Jesus. In 28:1-8 the women go to the right tomb and find it empty. When the tomb is found empty, the Jewish leaders concoct the story that Jesus' disciples stole his corpse (28:11-15). Thus Matthew emphasizes that the tomb was empty only because Jesus was raised from the dead.

Matthew also provides two appearance accounts, one to the women returning from the empty tomb (28:9-10) and the other to the eleven remaining apostles in Galilee (28:16-20). When the risen Jesus greets the women they "worship" him and he gives them the mission to tell the eleven to go to Galilee and meet him there. Then, in what is the climax of Matthew's gospel, the eleven apostles (minus Judas) "worship" the risen Jesus and he commissions them to carry on what he had begun during his earthly ministry: "make disciples of all nations, baptizing them . . . and teaching them . . ." (28:19-20a). And he promises to fulfill his role as "Emmanuel": "I am with you always, to the end of the age" (28:20b).

Reasons for Hope: The resurrection of Jesus is an event of the past. It took place in Jerusalem almost two thousand years ago. Those who went to his tomb on Easter Sunday found it empty, and they and many others came to believe that Jesus had been raised from the dead. The resurrection is also an event of the future. Jesus' resurrection is the basis of hope for all who hope for resurrection and eternal life. Because Jesus was raised, we can hope to be raised from the dead. Finally, it is also an event of the present. Through their baptism Christians have already begun to share in Jesus' resurrection and therefore should live in an appropriate manner. Thus the resurrection of Jesus is the basis, horizon, and dynamism of all Christian hope.

Part II

IMAGES OF HOPE IN PAUL'S LETTER TO THE ROMANS

Paul's letter to the Romans is a book of hope. It describes in various ways the hopes that have been fulfilled through Jesus' life, death, and resurrection, and it looks forward in hope to the full coming of God's kingdom and eternal life with God. Its key theological terms such as freedom, justification, reconciliation, and salvation all concern hopes already fulfilled and still to be fulfilled.

The focus of Paul's letter to the Romans is the gospel, that is, the good news (*euangelion* in Greek) of Jesus Christ, especially in his death and resurrection, and its consequences for human existence. Writing to a mixed community of Jewish and Gentile Christians, Paul sought to explain the significance of Jesus for all humans.

Paul was a founder of Christian communities. He took as his special vocation the task of bringing the gospel to non-Jews. His letters were generally addressed to communities he had founded, and they served as a way of providing continuing pastoral and theological advice to them. In fact, Paul is best understood as a pastoral theologian. Taking his starting point from the real problems of his communities, Paul brought to bear on them the theological insights he derived from the Christian tradition and from his own experience as a Jew and a Christian.

Paul, however, did not found the Christian community at Rome. Rather, Christianity arose there within the large Jewish community by the 40s of the first century C.E. There was a good deal of communication and travel between the Holy Land and Rome, and we can assume that Christianity came to Rome in the course of those contacts.

When he wrote his letter to the Romans, Paul had not yet visited Rome. Writing from Corinth in Greece around the year 57, Paul hoped to stop at Rome on his way to opening up a new mission in Spain. But before coming to Rome, Paul had first to bring the proceeds of his collection to Jerusalem.

These three places all are in the background of Paul's letter to the Romans. Paul sought to introduce himself to the Roman Christians and offer them his pastoral advice. He was also seeking to prepare a defense of his preaching of the gospel to non-Jews, something he knew he would have to present to the Jewish Christian leaders in Jerusalem. And he sought also to provide a synthesis of the gospel that he had been proclaiming and would proclaim in Spain. The thrust of the letter to the Romans is to explain how Jews and Gentiles alike can be part of God's people in Christ.

The good news ("gospel") of Jesus Christ is the central theme of this letter. After defining the gospel (1:1-17), Paul explains why all persons—Gentiles and Jews alike—need it (1:18–3:20) and how they can become part of God's people through faith after the pattern of Abraham (3:21–4:25). Next he considers how the gospel can bring freedom from the powers of Sin, Death, and the Law (5:1–7:25), and freedom for life in the Spirit (8:1-39). Then he reflects on God's plan of salvation history involving Jewish Christians like Paul, Gentile Christians, and other Jews (9:1–11:36). Finally he considers how the gospel should shape Christian life (12:1–13:14), how it can help in resolving community conflicts (14:1–15:13), and how the gospel may be promoted (15:14–16:27).

Paul's letters are the earliest complete documents in the New Testament. They were written between 51 C.E. (1 Thessalonians) and 57 C.E. (Romans). Thus they are older than the final forms of the four gospels (composed between 70 and 100 C.E.) and all the other books in the New Testament. They provide eloquent witness to the amazingly rapid and rich theological development of the Christian theological tradition. Within twenty or twenty-five years after Jesus' death, Christians were already speaking about him in exalted and sophisticated ways ("our Lord Jesus Christ"). The Pauline letters testify to what is perhaps better described as a theological explosion than as a development.

The focus of Paul's theology in the letter to the Romans is the death and resurrection of Jesus. He alludes only rarely in his letters to teachings and actions of the earthly Jesus. Even with regard to Jesus' death and resurrection, Paul was interested not so much in their historical details as in their significance for humankind. He regarded humankind before and apart from Christ as falling under the dominion of Sin, Death, and the Law. He interprets Christ's death "for us" as having broken that dominion and his resurrection as having made possible life in the Holy Spirit. And he looks forward to the time when the lordship of Christ will be recognized and celebrated by all creation.

Paul's letter to the Romans looks like a theological treatise, and to some extent it is. But it is first and foremost a real letter addressed to an early Christian community around 57 C.E. from Paul the apostle and pastoral theologian. Nevertheless, this letter has become a theological classic and captured the imagination of theologians throughout the centuries. The great twentieth-century theologian Karl Barth stated the matter correctly in my opinion: "If we rightly understand ourselves, our problems are the problems of Paul; and if we be enlightened by the brightness of his answers, those answers must be ours" (*The Epistle to the Romans*, 1).

The essays in this part of the book look at Paul's letter to the Romans as a document of hope. Indeed, there is no better expression of hope in the New Testament than Paul's own prayer in Rom 15:13: "May the God of hope fill you with all joy and peace in believing, so that you may abound in hope by the power of the Holy Spirit."

1. Gospel (Romans 1:1-7)

"The gospel concerning his Son, who was descended from David according to the flesh and was declared to be the Son of God with power according to the spirit of holiness by the resurrection from the dead, Jesus Christ our Lord." (Rom 1:3-4)

The word "gospel" derives from an Old English term ("godspel") that means "good news." The Greek word it renders is *euangelion*. Due to its prominence in the New Testament and early Christian literature, "gospel" has become almost synonymous with the life, death, and resurrection of Jesus and its saving significance in our lives. As the earliest writer in the New Testament, Paul used the word in the primitive sense of the good news about Jesus. Very soon, however, *euangelion* came to refer to narratives about the deeds and teachings of Jesus (Matthew, Mark, Luke, John).

Background: *Besora*, the Hebrew equivalent to *euangelion*, appears in the sense of "good news" about military victories in 2 Sam 4:10 and 18:22, 25. The verbal form ("to announce good news") is prominent in key passages in Second and Third Isaiah (40:9; 52:7; 60:6; 61:1). There the context is liberation from servitude during Israel's exile in Babylon (6th century B.C.E.) and the return to Israel's homeland. This usage gives a religious and redemptive tone to the appearances of *euangelion* in Paul's letters.

In the secular Greek of New Testament times, *euangelion* developed an association with the Roman emperors—with their births, birthday celebrations, accessions, and victories. A Greek inscription dated to 9 B.C.E., from Priene in Asia Minor (near Miletus), celebrates the birthday of the Roman emperor Augustus with these words: "the birthday of the god (= the emperor) was for the world the beginning of joyful tidings *(euangelia)* that have been proclaimed on his account." This usage suggests that there may also be a political overtone when *euangelion* occurs in the Pauline writings.

Paul: In the first words of his letter to the Romans, Paul describes himself as "an apostle set apart for the gospel of God." In describing his conversion to the risen Christ in Gal 1:13-17 Paul drew a close connection to his vocation or mission to proclaim Christ among non-Jews. Paul's conversion and his commission were inseparable. Both involved the gospel.

Most of Paul's letters were written to communities he had founded. He knew the people to whom he wrote, and what they had been taught. He used these letters to keep alive his personal relationship with them and provide them with ongoing pastoral and theological guidance.

Paul's letter to the Romans, however, is the great exception to Paul's usual practice. Paul had not introduced Christianity to Rome. Rather, it had already taken root there in the local Jewish community at a very early stage, probably from its contact with people from the "mother church" in Jerusalem. That meant that at the beginning of his long and bold letter to the Roman Christians Paul had to develop a common ground with them. He did so by quoting the very early summary of Christian faith (a "gospel") now preserved in Rom 1:3-4.

That this definition of the gospel was already a traditional summary is indicated by its un-Pauline language ("the spirit of holiness" rather than "the Spirit" or "the Holy Spirit") and perhaps even un-Pauline theology (it could imply that Jesus became the Son of God only at his resurrection from the dead).

Paul cited the formula presumably because both he and the Roman Christians knew it and regarded it as "the gospel." What mattered most was the basic content, not the details.

The summary of the gospel in Rom 1:3-4 makes three basic affirmations about Jesus of Nazareth: He is the Son of David/ Messiah, the Son of God, and the Lord. The infancy narratives in Matthew 1–2 and Luke 1–2 establish that, through Joseph, Jesus belonged to the house of David. At several points in his public ministry Jesus is hailed as "Son of David." In some Jewish circles the Messiah ("Anointed One") was expected to be a descendant of King David. The divine sonship of Jesus was hinted at in his many references to God as his "Father." That divine sonship became manifest most dramatically ("with power") in the resurrection of Jesus, and that event in turn led Paul and many other early Christians to believe that Jesus must have always been the Son of God. The title "Lord" *(kyrios)* was used in the Greek translation of the Old Testament to refer to God. To call Jesus "Lord," as many early Christians did, was to suggest his divinity.

Reasons for Hope: For Paul and other early Christians the risen Jesus was the primary image of hope and the basic reason for hope. The early summary of the gospel in Rom 1:3-4 emphasizes Jesus' roots in and continuity with his people Israel, the pivotal importance of his resurrection, and the high esteem in which he was held by believers (Messiah, Son of God, Lord). Most of Paul's letter to the Romans is a sustained reflection on the significance of Jesus' life, death, and resurrection, and their implications "for us." According to Paul the paschal mystery is not simply an event of the past. Rather, it shapes our hopes for the future and our lives in the present.

2. SALVATION (ROMANS 1:16-17)

"For I am not ashamed of the gospel; it is the power of God for salvation to everyone who has faith, to the Jew first and also to the Greek." (Rom 1:16)

For many people "salvation" is a religious or theological word that refers to success in the final judgment and happiness in the future life. However, the English verb from which it derives—"save," like its Hebrew *(yasha)* and Greek *(sōzō)* equivalents—has a much wider range. We may use that verb to describe how a firefighter saved a boy from burning, how a lifeguard saved a girl from drowning, or how an army saved a city from destruction.

Background: In the Bible "save" and "salvation" have a broad range of meanings. Individuals and peoples may be delivered from military attack, political oppression, physical illness, drowning, fire, or God's wrath. Israel's rescue from slavery in Egypt becomes the paradigmatic biblical experience of salvation within Israel's history. The return from the Babylonian exile in the 6th century B.C.E. is interpreted in light of the Exodus and at the same time is viewed as going beyond it ("a new heaven and a new earth"). After the exile there is a tendency to give more attention to the salvation of individuals and to put off salvation to the future, that is, to the final judgment accompanying the full coming of God's kingdom. At all times, however, the ultimate savior remains the God of Israel.

Paul: Romans 1:16-17 is generally regarded as the thesis statement or proposition of the entire letter to the Romans. It begins with a classic example of negative understatement *(litotes):* "For I am not ashamed of the gospel." By using two negatives ("not ashamed"), Paul in effect expresses his great enthusiasm for and total commitment to the gospel. For him, the gospel—the significance of Jesus' life, death, and resurrection—was the most important thing in his life and the main topic of his letter to the Romans.

Whereas in Rom 1:3-4 Paul's concern was with the good news about Jesus, here his focus shifts to what the gospel means for those who believe in it and make it their own. Paul describes the gospel as "the power of God," that is, a dynamic force that comes from God. The goal of this power is "salvation" for us, here understood in its ultimate religious sense as God's offer of rescue from future condemnation at the last judgment and the possibility of living in the present in right relationship with God and in freedom from the domination of Sin and Death. The paschal mystery (the gospel) allows us to find salvation in the future and to live in real freedom in the present.

As Paul will argue at length in what follows, all peoples—Gentiles (1:18-32) and Jews (2:1–3:20) alike—were "under the power of sin" (3:9). They could not save themselves. Only God could save them, and God did so through Jesus.

Faith is the means by which people can enter into the saving significance of the paschal mystery. Faith involves a basic trust and hope in God's justice (or righteousness) and covenant fidelity, as well as a recognition of the pivotal importance of Jesus' death and resurrection. This faith has both subjective and objective dimensions. It is the condition for participating in the power of the gospel. It is the proper response to the gospel.

The new order of salvation in and through Christ preserves to some extent the old order: "to the Jew first and also to the Greek." Jesus was a Jew who lived and worked almost entirely among his own people. Yet soon after his death the gospel about him was preached to and accepted by non-Jews (see Acts). In the new order, however, the saving significance of Jesus' death and resurrection is meant for all peoples. All of them needed the gospel, and the gospel is open to them all.

In Rom 1:17 Paul goes on to describe the gospel as the definitive revelation of the righteousness of God, that is, God's fidelity, loyalty, and fairness to all peoples. Those qualities, which pertain most obviously to the last judgment, also apply to the present. And again faith is the milieu ("through faith for faith") in which we can experience and participate in God's display of his justice or righteousness.

Reasons for Hope: Salvation is the ultimate Christian hope. It provides the horizon for all other hopes. It is not simply being rescued temporarily from danger, drowning, or fire.

It is being rescued definitively from the powers of Sin and Death. This hope is based on the paschal mystery—the life, death, and resurrection of Jesus. This hope is already a reality in the present. We experience it as freedom from the dominion of Sin and Death, and freedom for life in the Holy Spirit.

3. SACRIFICE (ROMANS 3:21-26)

"Whom God put forward as a sacrifice of atonement by his blood, effective through faith. He did this to show forth his righteousness because in his divine forbearance he had passed over the sins previously committed." (Rom 3:25)

Sacrifice means offering something precious to God. It can also describe giving up something good for some even greater good. For many people today sacrifice is a foreign concept. The "me generation" is not "into" sacrifice. Moreover, many people, especially women, feel that the concept of sacrifice has been unfairly imposed upon them in order to persuade them to do things that have turned out to be unnecessary or even harmful. When the term is understood positively, it is now generally used in ways that are spiritual (Lenten sacrifices) or metaphorical (giving one's life for others).

Background: In almost all the religions of the ancient world, material sacrifice was a central element. People came to temples or shrines and offered animals, crops, liquids, and other material goods to the gods. They did so out of respect for the gods, to achieve greater communion with the gods, and/or to atone or expiate for sins or faults committed against the gods, other persons, or the community.

The book of Leviticus is largely concerned with the sacrifices offered first in the priestly tabernacle and then at the Jerusalem Temple, and other matters related to them. In these sanctuaries Jews made peace offerings, holocausts, and sin offerings. A very important sacrifice took place every year in the fall on the Day of Atonement (Yom Kippur). According to Leviticus 16 the high priest presided over the sacrifice of bulls and goats, and then sprinkled animal blood within the Holy of Holies. The ritual was intended to wipe away the effects of sins committed by the people during the past year: "On this day atonement shall be made for you, to cleanse you; from all your sins you shall be clean" (Lev 16:30).

Paul: The text quoted at the beginning of this essay, Rom 3:25, is generally regarded as an early confession of Christian faith that Paul took over and made part of his own argument in Romans. The traditional confession first asserts that God put forward Jesus as "a sacrifice of atonement by his blood." The reference to the Jewish Day of Atonement ritual is clear. The language also fits in with the early Christian interpretation of Jesus' death as "for us" and "for our sins." Then it describes this sacrifice as evidence of God's willingness to forgive the sins of the past and offer a fresh start to humankind.

According to the earliest tradition Jesus' death was the one perfect sacrifice for sins, and it has made possible a new relationship between God and humans (justification). In the background of this theology is not only the Day of Atonement ritual but also the figure of the Suffering Servant ("he bore the sin of many and made intercession for the transgressors," Isa 53:12). The letter to the Hebrews is an extended meditation on the belief that Jesus as the great high priest offered himself as a sacrifice for our sins.

According to Paul such a sacrifice was necessary because "all have sinned and fall short of the glory of God" (Rom 3:23). In 1:18-32 Paul described how non-Jews refused to recognize the sovereignty of God in creation and so fell into a downward spiral of sin and depravity. In 2:1–3:20 Paul shows how Jews, despite having God's revelation in the Torah, also fell into captivity by Sin and Death.

The traditional confession about Jesus' sacrificial death in Rom 3:25 is at the heart of Paul's reflection on his place in God's plan of salvation in 3:21-26. It is surrounded by many of the great themes of Paul's theology: Christ as the manifestation of

God's righteousness or justice, the Jewish Scriptures as witnesses to Christ, grace or divine favor, faith as the proper human response, and the effects of the paschal mystery—justification, redemption, and forgiveness of sins. From this reflection Paul concludes in 3:28 that both Jews and Gentiles have been brought into right relationship with God not by their doing the works of the Old Testament Law but rather by imitating Jesus' fidelity to his heavenly Father and by the faith that has as its object the efficacy of Jesus' death and resurrection.

One of the factors that surprised and even scandalized both Jews and pagans was the early Christians' refusal to offer material sacrifices. According to the letter to the Hebrews, however, there was no more reason to do so, since Christ the great high priest had already offered himself as the one perfect sacrifice for sins: "We have been sanctified through the offering of the body of Jesus Christ once for all" (Heb 10:9). At the same time early Christians were extending the notion of sacrifice beyond the cultic sphere into all areas of life (see Rom 12:1; Heb 13:15).

Reasons for Hope: The sacrificial death of Jesus helps to explain why Christians can and should be people of hope. In Paul's view the situation of both Jews and Gentiles had become hopeless. They were unable to save themselves from sin and depravity. But the coming of Christ in the flesh, and especially his death and resurrection, meant a release from their captivity to the powers of Sin and Death and brought about the possibility of a new relationship with God that is expressed in terms such as redemption and justification.

4. Abraham (Romans 4:1-25)

"Hoping against hope, he [Abraham] believed that he would become
'the father of many nations,' according to what was said,
'So numerous shall your descendants be.'" (Rom 4:18)

The three great monotheistic religions—Judaism, Christianity, and Islam—all take Abraham as their "father" in faith.

Despite their many differences, each tradition finds in the figure of Abraham something that makes him a pivotal figure not only in its origin but also in its history and ongoing existence. That something is usually specified as "faith." However, in the case of Abraham there seems to be no sharp distinction between faith and hope. Abraham is as much an image of hope as he is an image of faith.

Background: In the book of Genesis, Abraham stands at the beginning of salvation history. He comes after some terrible events narrated in Genesis 1–11: the sin of Adam and Eve, Cain's murder of his brother Abel, the many evils leading up to the flood in the days of Noah, and the Tower of Babel episode. With the call of Abraham in Gen 12:1-3 to go forth from his homeland, God marks a new beginning. God promises to make Abraham into "a great nation" and to bless him and his descendants (12:2). God also promises to give him a son from his wife Sarah despite their old ages, and to make that son (Isaac) the vehicle by which the divine promises will be fulfilled.

Then in Genesis 22 God tests Abraham by commanding him to sacrifice Isaac. It would seem that if Abraham obeyed and killed Isaac, he would in effect be killing off the possibility of God's promises being fulfilled. Since Abraham shows himself obedient to God's command, God rescinds the command and reaffirms the promises. Throughout the pertinent episodes in Genesis, Abraham appears willing to accept God's word and to trust in God's power to turn his promises into realities. Abraham says "yes" to God's plans and thus shows himself to be an exemplary person of faith and hope.

Paul: In Rom 4:18 Paul describes Abraham as "hoping against hope." This phrase most likely alludes to the command to "sacrifice" Isaac in Genesis 22. Abraham's first and most fundamental hope was that through Isaac he would become "the father of many nations." Why then did Abraham not object or refuse to carry out God's command to sacrifice his son Isaac? Paul seems to suppose that Abraham expected that somehow God would make it possible for the promises to be fulfilled despite the apparent contradiction involved in sacrificing the very instrument (Isaac) by which they were to be fulfilled. Thus by "hoping against hope" Abraham became a model of hope in God's power to carry out his plan.

Abraham is very important to Paul's argument in Romans. Paul had already established that all people—Jews and Gentiles alike—needed the revelation of God's righteousness in Christ. In describing Jesus' death in terms of a sacrifice for sins (3:25), Paul had alluded to the sacrifice of Isaac in Genesis 22. What Paul wants to show in the rest of Romans is that through the paschal mystery it became possible for both Jews and Gentiles to be members of the people of God. They could become such on the basis of their faith, not the works of the Law. Thus Abraham provided the model for Paul's doctrine of justification by faith.

To establish his thesis of justification by faith, Paul points to Abraham's acceptance of God's promises about Isaac and many descendants through him in Gen 15:4-5. He takes very seriously the narrator's comment in Gen 15:6: "Abraham believed God, and it was reckoned to him as righteousness." Because of his faith and hope, Abraham was approved by God as "righteous" or "just," that is, in right relationship with God. That is what justification means.

Paul's point is that God dealt with Abraham in the realm of faith rather than works. He confirms this point by noting that God's declaration of Abraham's righteousness (Gen 15:6) preceded in time his circumcision (Gen 17:10-27) and occurred long before the giving of the Law to Moses on Sinai (Exodus 19–24). What matters, then, with regard to being just or righteous before God is faith (and hope), not circumcision or the works of the Law. What mattered most for Abraham was his conviction that "God was able to do what he had promised" (Rom 4:21). That is the essence of both faith and hope in the Bible.

Reasons for Hope: It has been said that hope is faith and love on pilgrimage. Abraham is the father not only of those who believe and love but also of those who hope. His example reminds us that hope involves a dialogue with God, and that people of hope manage to say "yes" to God as Abraham did— no matter how unlikely the circumstances may be. For Jews, Christians, and Muslims, Abraham should be an image of hope so that they can put aside past and present grievances and find in their father Abraham a way to move forward together in mutual understanding and hope.

5. JUSTIFICATION (ROMANS 5:1-11)

"Therefore, since we are justified by faith,
we have peace with God through our Lord Jesus Christ." (Rom 5:1)

When we try to "justify" ourselves we generally explain our actions in an effort to show that we have acted sincerely and have done nothing wrong. Sometimes we may even try to justify God when some natural disaster occurs. Defending God in the face of inexplicable evil and suffering is called "theodicy." But justification in its Pauline theological sense refers to God justifying humans. The image is that of a law court. The judge is God. In this case God the judge declares humans, even though they are guilty, to be acquitted and free to live in a new way.

Background: In late Old Testament books and early Jewish writings around Jesus' time, the image of the last judgment became increasingly prominent. In fact, it provided a solution to the question of theodicy: How can an omnipotent and just God allow innocent persons to suffer and wicked persons to prosper? The answer is that at the last judgment the omnipotence and justice of God will be fully manifested, and then the righteous will be vindicated and the wicked will be punished. An excellent example of this kind of apocalyptic thinking appears in the *Rule of the Community,* one of the Dead Sea scrolls. The pertinent passage (3:13–4:26) is the instruction that the community's spiritual leader was to put before the new members. It provided them with a worldview for understanding the past, present, and future. It begins by acknowledging the sovereignty of the "God of knowledge" who created humans to govern the world and appointed two spirits to rule until the last judgment. The schema may be summarized in one sentence: "All the children of righteousness are ruled by the Prince of Light and walk in the ways of light, but all the children of falsehood are ruled by the Angel of Darkness and walk in the ways of darkness" (3:20). But God has decreed that this struggle is only temporary, and that in God's own time (the "visitation") there will be an end to the Angel of Darkness and his followers, and vindication for the Prince of Light and his followers.

Paul: Something like this apocalyptic schema underlies Paul's theology in Romans and his understanding of justification and its effects in particular. Paul identifies Christ and his Holy Spirit as the Prince of Light, and Sin and Death as the Angel of Darkness. Those who are "in Christ" and are led by the Holy Spirit do the deeds of light. Those who remain under the rule of Sin and Death do the deeds of darkness. At the last judgment those who are in Christ will be vindicated, and the others will be condemned and punished.

The resurrection of Jesus, however, led Paul and other early Christians to modify the schema. In Jewish circles resurrection was understood to be a collective, end-time event. But Christians claimed that one person, Jesus of Nazareth, has already been raised from the dead to live in eternal glory. That meant that the divine "visitation" has already begun. Furthermore, for those who are "in Christ" the last judgment has been somehow anticipated, and their verdict is acquittal or justification. Of course, there will still be a last judgment. But for those who have remained faithful "in Christ" and have continued to do the deeds of light there will be no condemnation. For them eternal life has already begun.

In Rom 5:1-11 Paul reflects on the effects of the justification brought about through Jesus' life, death, and resurrection. He insists that faith is the way by which we can become part of this process: "we are justified by faith." The effects include peace with God, access to divine favor or grace, and hope of sharing in the glory of God (5:1-2). The last item is a reminder that the best is yet to come. Even experiences of suffering have positive value, since "suffering produces endurance, and endurance produces character, and character produces hope" (5:3-4).

On our own, we humans did not deserve justification. But "while we were still weak, at the right time Christ died for the ungodly" (5:6). That having been said, Paul resumes his list of the positive effects of Jesus' death and resurrection: salvation and reconciliation. Salvation is rescue from condemnation at the last judgment, and reconciliation is with God our Creator and Lord.

Reasons for Hope: The Christ-event is not simply past or future. It is also present. It has (or should have) effects in the lives of Christians today. With Jesus' resurrection the future judgment has broken into the present, and people of faith have been declared acquitted or justified. Their new beginning is hope fulfilled and opens up their horizons to even greater hopes. Through Christ we have peace with God, access to divine grace, hope of sharing in God's glory, salvation, and reconciliation with God. Even experiences of suffering should not discourage us, since they too can lead to our being better people of hope and to still greater hopes.

6. ADAM (ROMANS 5:12-21)

"But the free gift is not like the trespass. For if the many died through the one man's trespass, much more surely have the grace of God and the free gift in the grace of the one man, Jesus Christ, abounded for the many." (Rom 5:15)

The Hebrew word ʾ*adam* means "man" or "humankind." The term itself suggests that the man bearing the name Adam is an typical or even archetypical figure, someone who represents all of humankind. Adam is a major character only in Genesis 1–3, and is seldom mentioned elsewhere in the Old Testament. To some extent Adam owes his theological fame to Paul's meditation on Adam and Christ in Rom 5:12-21. There Adam is a negative example. But the result of his negative behavior is the superabundance of divine grace that came with Christ (*felix culpa* = "happy fault"). Through his connection with Christ, Adam becomes an image of hope.

Background: According to Gen 1:27, Adam was the crown of God's work of creation. He is said to have been made "in the image of God." According to Gen 2:16-17, God gave Adam an idyllic life in the Garden of Eden and set down only one rule: "of the tree of the knowledge of good and evil you shall not eat."

The biblical story of the "fall" or "original sin" in Genesis 3 seeks to explain why there is sin and death in the world. It describes how our first parents were enticed into disobeying God's single commandment and eating from the fruit of the tree in the middle of the garden. The serpent assured them that no harm would come to them ("you will not die"), that they would become like gods, and that they would know "good and evil." The catastrophic results of the disobedience of Adam and Eve included shame at nakedness, fear of snakes, pain in childbearing, and the need for hard physical labor. But the most disastrous effect is death: "you are dust, and to dust you shall return" (3:19). Adam ("the man") is condemned to return to the ʾadamah (the Hebrew word for "ground").

Paul: Paul's comparison of Adam and Christ in Rom 5:12-21 is the chief New Testament source for the doctrine of original sin. Paul presents Adam and Christ as archetypical figures. They both are bearers of a fate or destiny that affects all humans. But whereas the result of Adam's disobedience is the entrance of sin and death into the world, the result of Christ's obedience is divine grace and eternal life. Paul's point is captured by his statement in Rom 5:15: "But the free gift is not like the trespass." What Christ brought about is much more positive and hopeful than what Adam caused.

In Rom 5:12-14 Paul interprets Genesis 3 as describing the entrance of sin and death into the world through Adam's disobedience, and he suggests that all humans tend to repeat Adam's sin. The Jewish apocalypse known as 2 Baruch makes this point well: "Each of us has become our own Adam" (54:19). However, Paul does introduce a ray of hope with his description of Adam as "a type of the one who was to come." That one is Christ, and he is the bearer of a different kind of fate.

In Rom 5:15-19 Paul contrasts Adam and Christ on several counts. Whereas Adam's sin brought sin and death for "many" (= all), Christ's sacrificial death on the cross has become the source of superabundant grace for all (5:15). Whereas Adam's sin brought condemnation, Christ's death brought about justification (5:16). Whereas Adam's trespass initiated the reign of death, Christ's death issued in the reign of life (5:17). Whereas Adam's sin led to condemnation for all, Jesus' act of righteousness led to justification and life for all (5:18). Whereas Adam's disobedience made many into sinners, Jesus' obedience to his Father has made many righteous (5:19).

In his letters Paul expresses several positive views about the Old Testament Law. It is a witness to Christ, a guide or pedagogue for living wisely, and a source of wisdom. He insists that he upholds the Law. However, at times, as in Rom 5:20-21, he takes a negative approach and views the Law as a stimulus to sin and so an ally of sin and death. By specifying sins the Law attracts people to commit sins. Nevertheless, even here the logic of superabundance applies: "where sin increased, grace abounded all the more."

Reasons for Hope: Christian hope is possible because Jesus as the Second Adam has broken the dominion of Sin and Death over humankind. Through his sacrificial death Jesus has reversed the consequences of Adam's sin and made it possible for us to enjoy right relationship with God. Through the First Adam we became wounded and weak. Through the Second Adam we have become children of God and people of hope.

We can now legitimately hope for and realize what Adam and Eve imagined they could obtain by their sin: "you will be like God." We are indeed like God through the example and power of Jesus the Son of God. And so we can hope for eternal life with God and the fullness of God's reign.

7. DEATH AND LIFE (ROMANS 6:1-11)

"Therefore we have been buried with him for baptism into death, so that, just as Christ was raised from the dead by the glory of Father, so we too might walk in newness of life." (Rom 6:4)

The English word "baptism" derives from the Greek word *baptizein,* which refers to dipping (or even drowning or sinking) someone or something into water. Like water itself, baptism is an ambivalent symbol, conveying the ideas of death (dying by drowning) and life (renewing, cleansing, purifying).

Background: The Jewish precedents for Christian baptism include ritual purification undertaken by priests at the Jerusalem Temple, ritual baths, proselyte baptism, and John's baptism. Since Jesus underwent John's baptism and seems to have carried on John's ministry of preparation for the coming of God's kingdom, John's baptism appears to have been the most important precedent. It is possible that Jesus himself practiced John's rite of baptism (see John 3:22, 26; 4:1). What sets early Christian baptism apart from its predecessors (even John's baptism) was its being administered "in the name of Jesus" and its association with the gift of the Holy Spirit.

There is no explicit description of the ritual of baptism in the New Testament. From various clues, however, it seems that it followed some form of catechesis, was administered by another person, involved immersion where possible, and was carried out "in the name of Jesus" or "in the name of the Father, the Son, and the Holy Spirit." The ceremony was probably accompanied by hymns, confessions of faith, and the imposition of hands.

Paul: When referring to baptism in Rom 6:2-4, Paul exploits the symbolic ambivalence of water as both deathdealing and lifegiving. Taking up what was probably already a traditional interpretation, Paul emphasizes baptism as participation in both Jesus' death and his resurrection.

According to Paul, the act of being baptized meant entering in a kind of mystical way into the death of Jesus: "Do you not know that all of us who have been baptized into Christ Jesus were baptized into his death?" (6:3). At the same time baptism for Paul meant death to sin. In other words, it involved an end to the dominion of Sin over the baptized person as a power and the beginning of new life with Christ. Paul was trying to answer the charge (6:1) that since the new order initiated by Christ was so far superior to the old order of Adam it might be good to keep on sinning so that grace might abound all the more. Paul dismisses this bizarre suggestion by asserting that those who have died to Sin in baptism cannot and must not keep living in it. Dying with Christ in baptism means dying to Sin as one's lord.

Baptism, according to Paul, also and especially meant participation in the resurrection of Christ. Through baptism, eternal life has already begun. Just as baptism means dying to Sin, it also means dying to Death in the sense that Death no longer has dominion. In baptism there is a transfer of masters from Sin and Death to Christ. Just as Christ broke down the dominion of Sin and Death through his death and resurrection, so those who are baptized into Christ come to share in the benefits of his saving action.

Nevertheless, for Paul the fullness of resurrected life remains future: "if we have died with Christ, we believe that we will also live with him" (6:8). Resurrected life begins with baptism. Meanwhile, the challenge facing every Christian is to "walk in newness of life" (6:4). Baptized persons live between the times—between the time of domination by Sin and Death and the fullness of the reign of God. The term "walk" in the Bible evokes behavior or conduct that is appropriate to one's status as having been baptized into Jesus' death and resurrection. Paul summarizes his vision of Christian life as being "dead to sin and alive to God in Christ Jesus" (6:11). Present participation in Christ through baptism is the ground of hope for eternal life and the fullness of God's kingdom.

Reasons for Hope: In baptism we enter into the death of Christ (water as a symbol of death) and into the life of Christ (water as a symbol of life). Christian hope is based on union with Christ expressed in baptism. The ground of Christian hope is Jesus' death and resurrection. For every Christian, baptism is a pivotal moment because that is when full participation in the paschal mystery begins. Likewise, the baptism of every Christian is a reason for hope—hope for that person's walking in newness of life, and hope for the Christian community and the world in which the baptized person lives. The challenge facing all Christians is to take seriously their baptismal identification with Christ and to walk in newness of life.

8. THE DIVIDED SELF (ROMANS 7:7-25)

"Wretched man that I am!
Who will rescue me from this body of death?
Thanks be to God through Jesus Christ our Lord!" (Rom 7:24-25a)

People in antiquity did not write much about themselves in the first person singular mode ("I") that is so popular in our modern media. In the New Testament Paul is something of an exception, with his brief but eloquent descriptions of his earlier life in Judaism (Gal 1:13-17; Phil 3:4-16) and of his sufferings for the sake of the Gospel (2 Corinthians 10–13). In Rom 7:7-25, however, Paul uses a great amount of "I" language to describe the tensions of living both in the flesh and in the spirit. The "old Adam" is still alive in all of us, and Paul expresses the tension that implies.

Background: The late-first-century C.E. Jewish apocalypse known as 4 Ezra (= 2 Esdras 3–14) gives unusual attention to the figure of Adam and the effects of his "original sin." Not only did Adam's sin bring death to all his descendants (4 Ezra 3:7), but it also caused all of them to repeat Adam's experience: "Thus the disease became permanent; the law was in the hearts of the people along with the evil root" (3:22; see 3:26-27). According to 4 Ezra 7:11 Adam's sin brought condemnation upon the whole world—to the point that Ezra complains in 7:116-126 that it would have been better if God had not created Adam at all.

Paul: In Rom 7:7-13 Paul reflects on the negative aspect of the Old Testament Law, and how it effectively became an ally of Sin and Death. By objectifying and specifying sin ("you shall not covet"), the Law became a stimulus to sin. Of course, the Law was given to Moses long after Adam's sin. Nevertheless, the sin of Adam and Eve consisted in disobeying the one commandment God gave them: "of the tree of the knowledge of good and evil you shall not eat" (Gen 2:17). Thus Adam's sin of disobedience is paradigmatic or prototypical of every sin, including Paul's, as well as mine and yours.

The language of Rom 7:14-25 is in the present tense, suggesting that Paul speaks about his own present experience (as well as mine and yours). In 7:14-18 Paul acknowledges the division or tension within himself between his attraction to evil ("sold into slavery under sin") and his desire to do good. Indeed, he even feels possessed by Sin. Instead of a Christ-mysticism ("it is no longer I who live, but it is Christ who lives in me," Gal 2:20), he describes a type of Sin-mysticism ("sin that dwells in me," Rom 7:17). In 7:19-20 he underscores the plight of all those undergoing the struggle between their good and evil inclinations by a memorable saying: "For I do not do the good I want, but the evil I do not want is what I do" (7:19). Despite his good intentions he finds another "law" or principle at work within him that makes him captive to Sin and Death (7:21-23).

The only one who can rescue Paul (and us) from this "body of death" is "God through Jesus Christ our Lord" (7:25a). The positive point of Paul's meditation on the divided, conflicted self is to emphasize the importance of divine grace made manifest in Christ.

Reasons for Hope: The basic reason for hope, according to Paul, is God working through Christ. Left to our own devices as descendants of Adam, we would live under the dominion of Sin and Death, and even turn the natural law and the revealed Law of Moses into stimuli to sin. The only one who could rescue us from this wretched state is God working through Christ. In this sense Christian hope is supernatural, since our nature is fractured, if not corrupted. Because of the supernatural character of Christian hope, our natural hopes can be channeled in positive directions and we can find freedom from the tensions and conflicts Paul describes so memorably in Rom 7:7-25.

9. SPIRIT (ROMANS 8:1-17)

"For all who are led by the Spirit of God are children of God."
(Rom 8:14)

At the end of a hot spell, a cool wind is welcome. The Hebrew and Greek words for "wind" *(ruah* and *pneuma)* have wide ranges of meaning. They can refer to the wind outside us or the breath within us. In theological usage they can describe the human spirit or soul as well as the Holy Spirit through whom God continues to work in the world around us and within us. To add to the confusion, the ancient Hebrew and Greek manuscripts did not capitalize words. So it is often difficult to distinguish in the Bible between the human "spirit" and the Holy "Spirit."

Background: The ambiguity of "spirit" appears in the first two verses of the Bible. Should Gen 1:2 be rendered "a wind from God" or "the Spirit of God"? However, the "spirit of God" is clearly active in choosing ancient Israel's leaders and inspiring the prophets to speak to the people on God's behalf. In Luke's gospel (3:22) the Holy Spirit comes upon Jesus and remains with him throughout his public ministry. Taking over the language of Isa 61:1, Jesus in Luke 4:18 declares that the words "the Spirit of Lord is upon me" have been fulfilled in him. And in Acts 2, after the ascension of Jesus, the Holy Spirit comes "like the rush of a violent wind" upon the community gathered in Jerusalem and empowers them to continue the prophetic ministry of Jesus. In John 14–16 Jesus promises that the Holy Spirit under the title of "Paraclete" (advocate, counselor, defense attorney, etc.) will enable Jesus' disciples to remain faithful to his teachings and to adapt to new circumstances.

Paul: In Rom 8:1-17 Paul uses the word *pneuma* to refer to both the human spirit and the Holy Spirit. Here the "spirit" is that aspect of the person that is open to the workings of the Holy "Spirit." And the Holy Spirit in turn works with and guides the human spirits of those who are in Christ through baptism.

Whatever problems Paul had with the Old Testament Law, the root of his problem was that the Law could not do what only the Spirit of Christ could do: bring about right relationship with God (justification). Just as "spirit" refers to the person's openness to God, "flesh" in this context generally describes what in the person is opposed to and hostile to God (8:1-4). It is the Holy Spirit who can draw the person out of the conflict and tension described in Rom 7:7-25.

In Rom 8:5-8 Paul explains what it means to be in the "flesh." Those who are in the flesh set their minds on the things of the flesh and do the works of the flesh. They are led by Sin and Death, are hostile to God and God's Spirit, and cannot please God.

In Rom 8:9-11 Paul explains what it means to live in the "spirit/Spirit." Those in whom the Spirit dwells find life and right relationship with God. It is striking to look at the several different ways in which Paul describes the Holy Spirit in 8:9-11: the Spirit of God, the Spirit of Christ, the Spirit, the Spirit of the one who raised Jesus from the dead, and his Spirit. These various expressions played important roles in formulating the Christian doctrines of the Holy Spirit and the Trinity.

After reminding the Romans that living by the flesh brings death and living by the Spirit brings life (8:12-13), Paul affirms that "all who are led by the Spirit of God are children of God" (8:14). Thus he suggests that we are drawn along by the Spirit's promptings, and that we share in the divine filiation Jesus enjoys as the Son of God. As adopted children of God, we too can call upon God as "Abba! Father!" (8:15). And the Holy Spirit working with our spirits bears witness that we are God's children—provided that we are willing to enter fully into both the suffering and the glory of Christ (8:16-17).

Reasons for Hope: The Holy Spirit enables Christians to move forward in the present and into the future as people of hope. We are assured that the Holy Spirit dwells within us and empowers us to connect with the Father and the Son. The Holy Spirit assures us that we are God's children and we can approach God as a loving parent with confidence and trust. Nevertheless, Paul also reminds us that even in our life in the Spirit suffering may be a reality, and so he puts a condition on life in the Spirit: "if, in fact, we suffer with him so that we may be glorified with him" (Rom 8:17).

10. Childbirth (Romans 8:18-39)

> *"We know that the whole creation has been groaning in labor pains until now."* (Rom 8:22)

In every age, but especially in biblical times, the birth of a child was (and is) a source of great joy and celebration. However, childbirth is also a painful and dangerous event. Then as now the gestation period had to run its course before a healthy child could be born. The rate of infant mortality in biblical times was very high, and often young women did not survive giving birth.

Background: Genesis 3:16 interprets the pain that women undergo in giving birth as an effect of the sin of Adam and Eve.

In the New Testament the image of childbirth is associated with the birth of the Messiah (Rev 12:2) and the full coming of God's kingdom. In the eschatological discourse in Matthew 24:8 (see Mark 13:8), Jesus speaks about the cosmic disturbances related to the Day of the Lord as "but the beginning of the birthpangs." The plea for sustenance in the time of testing mentioned in the Lord's Prayer (Matt 6:13) recognizes that the full coming of God's kingdom may be painful and dangerous, that God will bring about his kingdom according to his own schedule, and that in the end it will be a source of great joy and celebration. In his farewell discourse in John 16:21, Jesus compares the sufferings that he and his followers were to endure during the Passion to what a woman goes through in delivering her child.

Paul: In Romans 8:18-19 Paul claims that the sufferings of the present pale into insignificance in comparison with the glory that is about to be revealed. In 8:20-21 he includes all creation in the present sufferings. Here Paul describes the full coming of God's kingdom in terms of childbirth: "the whole creation has been groaning in labor until now." What is distinctive is that the whole of creation, not just the Messiah or humankind, is involved in the process of cosmic redemption. He looks forward in hope to its liberation from futility and decay, along with the definitive manifestation of the children of God. According to 8:22-23 there is a kind of sympathetic relationship between the children of God and creation itself as they await their vindication. Both are involved in a painful and dangerous process. The process will reach its goal in God's own time. And both can hope for a productive and joyous result.

The image of childbirth as a way of describing the full coming of God's kingdom leads Paul into a short reflection on the nature of hope in 8:24-25. Just as the Romans found their way to Christian faith in hope, so too they should look forward to the definitive display of God's kingdom in hope. What we hope for, we do not yet see—like the child still in the womb.

What we hope for, we await with patience—like the child who must come to term and be born in due time.

The remainder of Romans 8 gives further reasons for hope. According to 8:26-27, the Holy Spirit helps us in our weakness and intercedes for us with the Father. This assistance is part of the "first fruits of the Spirit" (8:23) that comes with baptism. Moreover, according to 8:28-30, God has a plan for those who love God, and will care for them at every step of the way. Being "conformed to the image of his Son," Christians can look forward to sharing in the glory of the Son in God's kingdom.

It has been said that the fundamental question of Christian spirituality is, Do you trust God? In 8:31 Paul asserts that the ground of Christian hope is the firm conviction that "God is for us." Because God is for us, nothing—neither physical sufferings nor cosmic powers—can "separate us from the love of God in Christ Jesus our Lord" (8:39).

Reasons for Hope: In Romans 8, Paul gives many reasons for trusting God. But the most basic reason is God working in Christ: "He who did not withhold his own Son, but gave him up for us all, will he not with him also give us everything else?" (8:32). In baptism we come to share in the paschal mystery, and we look forward to "the glory about to be revealed to us" (8:18). Like a woman about to give birth, we recognize that pain and danger may lie before us. And we know that we must wait patiently for God to do what only God can do: "Thy kingdom come!" As people of hope we wait, convinced that God is for us, and that the joy associated with the glory to be revealed far outweighs our present sufferings.

11. REMNANT (ROMANS 9:1-29)

"And Isaiah cries out concerning Israel, 'Though the number of the children of Israel were like the sand of the sea, only a remnant of them will be saved.'" (Rom 9:27)

A remnant is a leftover or survivor. Pieces of cloth left over from making dresses or suits are sometimes called "remnants." The word can be used with reference to practically anything. When applied to a people or group, a remnant is what remains after a disaster or catastrophe. It can also refer to what may be the nucleus for a possible future rebuilding of the people or group. In that sense a remnant may be an image of hope.

Background: The idea of a remnant appears early in the Bible and runs through it. Noah and his family (Genesis 6–8), Lot after the destruction of Sodom (Genesis 18–19), and Moses and the Hebrews after escaping from Egypt (Exodus) all constitute what can be called a remnant. Among the prophets the "remnant" referred to those in Israel who accepted their warnings and repented from their evil ways. The prophet Isaiah named one of his sons "Shearjashub," which in Hebrew means "a remnant shall return." According to Mic 2:12 the Lord promises: "I will surely gather you, O Jacob, I will gather the survivors of Israel." Here the remnant becomes Israel.

The people who gave us the Dead Sea scrolls regarded themselves as the remnant of the "true" Israel and viewed other Jews (like the Pharisees) as not belonging to the real people of God. For John the Baptizer it was not enough for Jews to appeal to their status as children of Abraham in the face of the coming kingdom of God (Matt 3:9; Luke 3:8). The circle of twelve apostles (with its evocation of the twelve tribes of Israel) that Jesus assembled suggests that he regarded his own group as the remnant within Israel.

Paul: In his long and complex meditation on God's saving plan for humankind in Romans 9–11, Paul identifies Jewish Christians like himself as the remnant of the people of God. He does so by combining two texts from Isaiah ("only a remnant of them will be saved," Isa 10:22-23; and "if the Lord of hosts had not left survivors to us," Isa 1:9) in Rom 9:27-29. Thus he sees God's will made known in the Scriptures as being fulfilled in his own time. As in the Old Testament, the remnant is an image of hope not only for the church but also for historic Israel.

Paul's use of the "remnant" image needs to be put in the context of his argument in Rom 9:1-29. According to 9:1-5, Paul was discouraged at the unwillingness of many of his fellow Jews to accept the Gospel. Nevertheless, he saw clearly that in the history of salvation Israel always retained the prerogatives of being a special people to God: "the adoption, the glory, the covenants . . . the Messiah" (9:4-5). Later in the argument Paul asserts that "the gifts and calling of God are irrevocable" (11:29). Paul could not imagine the people of God without a root in historic Israel.

Nevertheless, Paul still had to explain why many of his fellow Jews were rejecting the Gospel while many non-Jews were accepting it. It might seem that "the word of God had failed" (9:6). Paul first appeals in 9:6-13 to God's ways of acting in patriarchal times, when God preferred Isaac to Abraham's other sons and chose Jacob over Esau. Paul's theological principle is the remnant idea: "not all Israelites truly belong to Israel" (9:6).

In 9:14-18 Paul defends God's freedom to use whatever instruments he wishes, even Pharaoh in the Exodus, to show mercy to his people. Then in 9:19-21 he evokes the analogy of the potter shaping clay into various objects, some precious and others ordinary. The point is that we cannot dictate to God how God should deal with his people.

But how could non-Jews be part of God's people? Again Paul appeals to Israel's own Scriptures. He interprets Hos 2:23 ("not my people I will call my people") and 1:10 ("not my people . . . shall be called children of the living God") to refer not to rebellious Israel (as in Hosea) but rather to those Gentiles who were becoming part of God's people by their association with the Jewish Christian remnant represented by Paul and his Jewish coworkers.

Reasons for Hope: The remnant of Jewish Christians like Paul were the nucleus from which the church as the people of

God has been built and expanded to include all nations. The Gentile Christians were in a sense honorary Jews incorporated into the people of God through Jesus the Jew. Without the remnant made up of Christian Jews like Paul there would be no continuity between historic Israel and the church. The church would have no reason to claim to be the people of God. The church needs always to recover its Jewish roots and to shape its identity in the light of God's promises to his people Israel. Without the remnant there would be no church.

12. OLIVE TREE (ROMANS 11:17-26A)

"But if some of the branches were broken off,
and you, a wild olive shoot,
were grafted in their place to share the rich root of the olive tree,
do not boast over the branches." (Rom 11:17-18a)

Olive trees are indigenous to western Asia, including Palestine. While they can be grown from seeds, they are frequently grafted from older trees. They have extensive root systems. They are slow in growing but reach heights of more than twenty feet. The "wild" olive tree is probably a separate species rather than simply a tree left unpruned. The olive tree may produce fruit for hundreds of years. Its fruit can be eaten or crushed to produce olive oil. The oil was used in cooking as well as in medicines, fuel for lamps, and cosmetics. The wood from the olive tree is strong and beautiful, and was used in the Jerusalem Temple.

Background: According to Deut 7:13 olive oil, grain, and wine were among the most important products of the Holy Land. The olive tree and its oil symbolized fertility, beauty, usefulness, and dignity. Olive oil was used in rituals including the anointing of priests, prophets, and kings. The Hebrew word "Messiah" derives from the verb "to anoint," and the Greek equivalent for "Anointed One" is *Christos* ("Christ"). In Jer 11:16 the olive tree is a symbol for Israel as the people of God:

"The LORD once called you, 'A green olive tree, fair with goodly fruit'" (see also Hos 14:6).

Paul: In Romans 9–11 Paul was trying to fathom God's plan of salvation, involving Jewish Christians like himself, Gentile Christians, and non-Christian Jews. He regarded himself and other Jewish Christians as the remnant of the people of God. He viewed Gentile Christians as now an integral part of the people of God through their new faith in the God of Israel and Jesus the Jew. He was still seeking to find a place for other Jews in this schema. But he was convinced that God the faithful and merciful one still had a plan for the rest of Israel.

In Rom 11:17-24 Paul develops the image of the olive tree both to summarize his findings thus far and to make a place for his fellow Jews who had not accepted the Gospel. He addresses the analogy to Gentile Christians who seem to have considered themselves superior to Jews. He reminds them that their own present dignity as part of God's people is based on their newfound relationship to historic Israel, and that God still has a plan for all Israel in the future.

In order to put the Gentile Christians in their proper place, Paul identifies them in 11:17-18 as wild olive shoots that had been grafted onto the rich root of the olive tree (the Jewish Christian remnant). He equates those Jews who are not part of the remnant with branches that have been broken off from the olive tree. He warns the Gentile Christians to remember that the root (Israel as the historic people of God) supports them, and not vice versa.

According to 11:19-22 the Gentile Christians are partly correct in assuming that they have taken the place of the non-Christian Jews on the olive tree. And Paul admits that those branches have been broken off because of their lack of faith, and that the Gentile Christians have been grafted on because of their faith. He interprets these developments in terms of God's justice and mercy, the two great biblical attributes of God. And he warns the Gentile Christians that they too can be cut off unless they persist in faith.

Nevertheless, according to 11:23-24 there is still hope for non-Christian Jews. It is always possible that God, who has cut them off from the olive tree, will graft them back on. Indeed, he notes, it is easier to graft natural branches back onto the olive tree than it was to graft branches from a wild olive tree onto the original stock. In other words, it will be easier for non-Christian Jews to become part of the olive tree again than it was for Gentile Christians to be made part of it in the first place.

Reasons for Hope: The olive tree is a hope-filled image of the people of God. Paul used it to explain God's fidelity to his people Israel and his mercy toward non-Jews. Paul's ultimate hope is that all three entities—the Jewish Christian remnant, the Gentile Christians, and other Jews—will eventually be united into the one people of God. Paul firmly believed that God will bring this to pass, and so in 11:25-26a he reveals the "mystery" of God's plan for the salvation of all three entities: "a hardening has come upon part of Israel, until the full number of the Gentiles has come in. And so all Israel will be saved."

13. BODY (ROMANS 12:1-8)

"For as in one body we have many members, and not all the members have the same function, so we, who are many, are one body in Christ, and individually we are members of one another."
(Rom 12:4-5)

The image of the body is easy enough to grasp. We each have a body. We know that when every part of our body is healthy and functioning properly we are generally happy and productive. But if one part (an arm or leg, for example) is injured and gives us pain, our life becomes difficult and unpleasant.

Background: The body is a natural symbol, and so the search for a specific biblical or historical background is not especially useful. However, the Old Testament concept of corporate personality ("all Israel") and the Greco-Roman metaphor of the city as a body ("the body politic") may well have contributed to the Pauline image. Jesus' words at the Last Supper over the bread ("This is my body that is for you," 1 Cor 11:24; Luke 22:19) make the link between Jesus, his "body," and the Christian community.

Paul: In 1 Corinthians 12–14 Paul provides a lengthy treatment of the church as the body of Christ. This image was especially appropriate for instructing a young Christian community with its many factions and pastoral problems. In Rom 12:4-5 he employs the same image in his introduction to the hortatory part of the latter chapters (12–15). There were, of course, factions and pastoral problems among the Roman Christians also, as chapters 14–15 show. The introductory passage as a whole (12:1-8) provides a remarkably positive and hopeful vision of Christian life.

When Paul gives practical advice to his readers he prefers the language of "appeal" or "exhortation" to that of "command." In Rom 12:1 he asks the Romans to present their "bodies" as a living sacrifice. Here he uses "body" in its biblical sense of the whole person (not just the "flesh"), especially in relationship with God and other persons. He urges his readers to view their everyday life in its entirety as the "place" for worshiping God (that is, worship should not be confined to a temple or church). Moreover, he challenges them to regard themselves as already living in the world (or "age") to come as opposed to this world (or "age"). Just as Jesus' resurrection has inaugurated the age to come, so those who are "in Christ" can and should live as already participating in the age to come.

In 12:3 Paul appeals to the "grace" given to him as an apostle and urges the Roman Christians to respect one another and avoid comparing themselves or competing with one another. The reason is that all Christians live "according to the measure of faith that God has assigned." This leads to a brief consideration of the church as the body of Christ.

In 12:4 Paul uses the "body" image in its obvious sense of encouraging harmony and cooperation within a group or community: "for just as in one body we have many members, and not all the members have the same function . . . ." Any leader or coach today could say the same. But in 12:5 Paul gives the image its distinctive Christian theological depth: "so we, who are many, are one body in Christ, and individually we are members one of another." The key phrase is "in Christ." What brings all these different people together—Jews and Gentiles, slaves and free, male and female—is their relationship to Christ. Christ makes the body and makes us members of one another. We are one body "in Christ."

As members of the body of Christ, all Christians have gifts (*charismata*) and are to use them for the good of others. In 12:6a Paul summarizes his teachings on the charisms: "We have gifts that differ according to the grace given to us." The seven gifts he lists in 12:6b-8 are not offices, nor are they exhaustive or listed in any obvious order of importance. Rather, they are concrete ways—prophecy, ministry, teaching, exhortation, generosity, leadership, compassion—in which Christians can and do build up the community as the body of Christ.

Reasons for Hope: Paul's vision of Christian life and the church in Rom 12:1-8 is full of hope. It reminds us that as baptized Christians we already live in the age to come, that the risen Christ has brought us together and made us into members of his body, and that as people with different gifts from the Holy Spirit we must use them for the common good. Those who take up these challenges will themselves be people of hope and signs of hope to others.

14. NIGHT AND DAY (ROMANS 13:11-14)

"The night is far gone, the day is near. Let us then lay aside the works of darkness and put on the armor of light." (Rom 13:12)

Night and day are as primordial a set of images as any in human experience. We all know night and day. Frequently these images are invested with moral significance. In daylight one expects at least good behavior, whereas in the dark of night anything goes. "Under cover of night" suggests deceptive or criminal activity, while "in broad daylight" indicates incredible boldness in the face of many witnesses. In the age before electricity the contrasts between day and night and between light and dark were much more striking and absolute than twenty-first-century people can imagine.

Background: The images of day and night and of light and darkness are all over the Bible. According to Gen 1:3, God's first words in the creation account are "Let there be light." Among the prophets "the day of the Lord" functions as an image of divine judgment and salvation. While at first applied to some imminent moment in Israel's history, the concept of the day of the Lord was eventually put off until the definitive display of God's sovereignty in the full coming of God's reign. Likewise, some Jews in Jesus' time (as seen especially in the Dead Sea scrolls) viewed the present as a struggle between the Prince of Light (Michael?) and the Angel of Darkness (Satan?). In the course of this struggle the children of light do the deeds of light (good), and the children of darkness do the deeds of darkness (evil).

Paul: The images of the day of the Lord and of the deeds of light are essential for understanding Paul's ethical teachings. These teachings are not ethical in the sense of timeless principles or truths applicable to all humans. Rather, they flow from the significance of Jesus' death and resurrection and are part of Paul's Christian virtue ethics.

The three major concerns of virtue ethics can be expressed in the form of three questions: Who am I? What is my goal or end in life? and How do I get there? Paul's answers (and those of every Christian) are shaped by his experience of the risen Christ on the road to Damascus. They would go something like this: I am now a child of God through Christ. My goal is eternal life with Christ in the reign of God. What I must do now are the deeds of light, that is, those actions from Scripture, tradition, human experience, and conscience that are appropriate for those who are seeking God's reign.

The context of Paul's use of the day-night/light-darkness imagery is the ethical section of his letter to the Romans (12:1–15:13). Having laid the theological foundations in 12:1-8, Paul offers advice on love toward others (12:9-21), Christian life under the Roman empire (13:1-7), and the love command (13:8-10). Then in 14:1–15:13 he brings to bear the power of the Gospel on some concrete pastoral problems that were dividing the Christians at Rome.

The content of Rom 13:11-14 involves the coming of God's reign and the stance of constant vigilance in conduct that it demands. In 13:11-12a Paul uses the images of waking from sleep and of the dawning of the day to show how close the day of the Lord is. He depicts life before and apart from Christ in terms of sleep and darkness, whereas life in Christ is wakefulness and light. In 13:12b-13 he urges his readers to "lay aside the works of darkness," that is, to avoid those vices and behaviors that are not consistent with life in Christ. Then he alludes to the image of Christian life as a military combat against the Prince of Darkness: "put on the armor of light." In 13:13 Paul contrasts living honorably "as in the day" with examples of living in the night: "not in reveling and drunkenness, not in debauchery and licentiousness, not in quarreling and jealousy." Finally, in 13:14 he contrasts putting on the Lord Jesus Christ (in baptism) and gratifying the desires of the flesh (life apart from Christ).

Reasons for Hope: Christians should know who they are (God's children through Christ), and that they already live in the light and in the day of the Lord. They should also know that their goal is life with God in the fullness of God's kingdom, and they should know what kinds of virtues, attitudes, values, and actions are appropriate to their identity and their goal. Paul gives examples of what is and is not consistent with that identity and that goal. Along with other New Testament writers, Paul takes the reign of God as the horizon of Christian ethical teaching and promotes a spirit of constant vigilance. This vigilance, however, is inspired not by fear but by hope. So Paul concludes his ethical teaching with a prayer of hope: "May the God of hope fill you with all joy and peace in believing, so that you may abound in hope by the power of the Holy Spirit" (15:13).

15. HOUSE (ROMANS 16:1-16, 21-23)

"Greet Prisca and Aquila, who work with me in Christ Jesus . . . .
Greet also the church in their house." (Rom 16:3a, 4a)

The family and the place where the family lives (a house) are the foundations of human life and society. The house, however humble, is where members of the family unit eat and sleep, where children are nurtured and educated, and where people entertain and interact with others. While most persons in New Testament times lived in modest circumstances, some relatively wealthy persons had large houses where not only their nuclear family dwelt but also their parents, servants, and slaves were present.

Background: Early Christians did not have temples or even special buildings set aside for worship. Instead they met at the private houses of members who were willing and able to host such gatherings. The most such a house could accommodate was probably about forty or fifty persons. Since Christians did not offer material sacrifices and gathered for Scripture readings, prayers, and the Lord's Supper, their worship needs could be satisfied by meeting in private homes (see Philemon 2, 2 John 10). The practice of meeting in houses led to the household as an early image of the church (see 1 Tim 3:15; Eph 2:19-22; Heb 3:1-6). While women must have played essential roles in the house churches, these communities probably also reflected the hierarchical and patriarchal assumptions of ancient Mediterranean societies (see Col 3:18–4:1; Eph 5:21–6:9).

Paul: Romans 16 seems for the most part to be a list of names. Writing from Corinth, Paul sends greetings to the Christians at Rome whom he knows. At least some of these people Paul encountered when they and other Jews were expelled from Rome under the emperor Claudius between 49 and 54 C.E. Two such persons were a married couple named Aquila and Prisca (or Priscilla; see Acts 18:1-2). According to Rom 16:3 they had "risked their necks" for Paul, presumably at Corinth. When Paul wrote to the Romans, Prisca and Aquila had returned to Rome, and their house had become a center for the local Christian community. (There may have been more than one.) And so Paul sends greetings to them and to "the church in their house" (16:5a).

The list of names in Romans 16 reveals much information about early Christian life that may also be signs of hope for our church today. Paul describes many persons on the list as "relatives" or "kin," presumably his fellow Jewish Christians. There are also many non-Jewish names (see 16:15, for example: Philologus, Julia, Nereus, and Olympas), which suggest a mixed community made up of both Jewish and Gentile Christians.

Many of the names on the list (Prisca, Mary, Junia, Tryphaena, Tryphosa, etc.) are clearly feminine, indicating the presence and prominence of women in the Roman church. One of these women (Junia) is described as "prominent among the apostles" (16:7). While she and her husband Andronicus may simply have had good reputations before the apostles, most interpreters today contend that Junia and Andronicus were both recognized as "apostles" in their own right.

At several points in his list Paul refers to certain men and women as his "coworkers" (16:3, 9, 12). One such coworker was Phoebe (16:1-2), who is called a "deacon" *(diakonos)* of the church of Cenchreae (the port of Corinth). It is likely that Phoebe had been commissioned to bring Paul's letter from Corinth to the

Christian community at Rome. In 16:21 Paul also mentions his co-worker Timothy as well as his fellow Jewish Christians (Lucius, Jason, Sosipater) at Corinth. In 16:22 Tertius, the scribe who was writing down Paul's letter, breaks in and sends his personal greetings. And in 16:23 Paul conveys greetings from "Gaius, who is host to me and the whole church" at Corinth, as well as Erastus (the city treasurer) and Quartus. These men were probably (at least relatively) rich and prominent.

Reasons for Hope: The list of names in Romans 16 is a sign of hope for Christians in all ages. What emerges from careful inspection of this list is a rich mixture of rich and poor, men and women, Jews and Gentiles, and (very likely) slaves and free persons. There is also a sense of many "coworkers" actively participating in and contributing to church life and to the Pauline mission. Paul did not work alone. From the start ministry in the church was collaborative. Paul's example is a sign of hope for the church today.

Part III

IMAGES OF HOPE IN THE BOOK OF REVELATION

T he book of Revelation, also known as the Apocalypse, is difficult reading for many people today. It is full of strange characters, mysterious numbers, and apparent violence. It has been used to justify all kinds of interpretations, beliefs, and practices. The simple fact, however, is that Revelation is a book of hope.

The hope that Revelation promotes is based on the resurrection of Jesus and the promises of God. It was originally addressed to Christians facing hostility and persecution. Its theology is not far from that of the Lord's Prayer (Matt 6:9-13; Luke 11:2-4). It looks forward to the full coming of God's reign and asks for divine sustenance and protection in the present tribulations and those to come. It seeks to impart courage and hope to suffering people as they await the second coming of Christ and fullness of life in the New Jerusalem. It has been said that only people in apparently "hopeless" situations can really understand this book.

More than any other New Testament book, Revelation is a book of images. Many of these come from the Old Testament, while some others reflect ancient Near Eastern and Greco-

Roman myths. But in Revelation these images are never exactly the same as they are in their sources, since they become transformed in the light of Jesus' life, death, and resurrection. The process has been aptly described as the "rebirth of images." Revelation provides many images of hope for its first readers and for us today.

The author's name was John, though he is probably not the same as the persons who wrote John's gospel or the Johannine epistles. This John had been exiled to the island of Patmos, off the western coast of Asia Minor (present-day Turkey), for preaching the Gospel. He was of Jewish origin, knew the Scriptures and apocalyptic traditions very well, and wrote in a kind of Semitic Greek. He was familiar with the pastoral situations of the seven churches in western Asia Minor for and to which he wrote. His book derives from his experience of the risen Christ that took place on Patmos on a Sunday. Its composition is generally dated to the end of the emperor Domitian's reign (95–96 C.E.), though it may incorporate earlier material from Nero's time.

Through his book John sought to provide hope for suffering Christians. The occasion seems to have been the persecution (or threat of one) that faced members of Christian communities in western Asia Minor. The persecution was a result of a program promoted by a local religious and/or political official (see 13:11-12) to force all inhabitants to participate in the worship of the Roman emperor as a god and of the goddess Roma as a symbol of the empire. Those who supported these imperial cults regarded Domitian as their "Lord and God." For Christians, however, such talk was blasphemy, and many of them could not in good conscience participate in this worship. John wrote to encourage such persons to remain faithful to their resolve, no matter what the consequences (even death) might be. These Christians were also experiencing hostility from the local Jewish communities as well as divisions within their own churches provoked by those whom John regarded as false teachers.

Revelation is an apocalypse that is a prophecy in the form of a letter. It is an apocalypse (like the book of Daniel) in that it is a revelation about the future and the heavenly realm. It is a prophecy in that John is commissioned to speak on God's behalf about the present and the future. It is a letter to be circulated as an encyclical to the seven churches addressed individually in chapters 2 and 3. And it was intended to be read aloud in each community: "Blessed is the one who reads aloud the words of prophecy, and blessed are those who hear and who keep what is written in it; for the time is near" (1:3).

The number "seven" is prominent in the structure of Revelation. The book is addressed to the seven churches, and in chapters 2 and 3 there are seven letters to the individual churches. Then there are three series of seven members (septets) presented under the images of seven seals (6:1–8:1), seven trumpets (8:7–11:19), and seven bowls (16:1-21). There are also seven eschatological events in chapters 19–21, and seven beatitudes are scattered throughout the book. The climax of the book is God's triumph over Babylon (= Rome) and the arrival of the New Jerusalem.

Revelation is a challenge to the imagination. It should not be left in the first century as a mere historical curiosity, nor should it be taken as a detailed forecast of future events. Rather, it is best read as a book of Christian hope based on Jesus' resurrection and God's promises to his people. It encourages confidence in God's plan and fidelity in the present. It is a book about Christian hope expressed chiefly through striking images.

While Revelation is mainly a book of hope, its very violent imagery disturbs many readers today—and rightly so! Perhaps the book's violence can be put into context by remembering that John stood in the literary tradition of Jewish apocalyptic imagery, that he wrote from the perspective of marginal persons who had been or were soon to be victims of violence, that he was convinced of the sinful character of much of the world around him, that he called upon God (and not his fellow Christians!) to be the ultimate agent of judgment and punishment, and that he produced a work of religious imagination (and not a battle plan).

1. ONE LIKE A SON OF MAN (REVELATION 1:12-20)

"And in the midst of the lampstands I saw one like the Son of Man, clothed with a long robe and with a golden sash across his chest."
(Rev 1:13)

The biblical expression "Son of Man" can be a way of referring to any human being. In some cases one could substitute "Son of Adam," since the term intends to suggest an identification with humankind in general. However, the conjunction "like" also suggests that this figure is somehow different from and more than an ordinary human. In the gospels the title "Son of Man" appears in three contexts. It is either a generic term for humans or a way of saying "I," or Jesus' way of referring to himself in the Passion predictions (see Mark 8:31; 9:31; 10:33-34), or a reference to the risen Jesus as a glorious figure who will preside over the last judgment (see Matt 25:31-46).

Background: The inaugural vision of the risen Christ in Rev 1:12-20 is a pastiche of biblical phrases and images. Even though John takes all these images from the Old Testament he never quotes the biblical text directly and almost always changes the images slightly when applying them to the risen Christ. The seven golden lampstands allude to the golden lampstand described in Exod 25:31-40 and to the golden lampstand with seven lamps on it in Zech 4:1-2. The glorious figure of the risen Christ is reminiscent of the brilliant appearance of the angel Gabriel in Dan 10:5-6. His identity as "one like the Son of Man" alludes to the figure in Dan 7:13 (Michael?) who is "given dominion and glory and kingship." And the notice that his head and hair were "white as white wool, white as snow" is reminiscent of the "Ancient One" in Dan 7:9.

John: The vision of the risen Christ described in Rev 1:12-20 is the foundational religious experience for everything that follows in the book. The vision (see 1:9-11) takes place on a Sunday ("the Lord's day") on the island of Patmos, off the coast of western Asia Minor, about sixty miles southwest of Ephesus.

John was there undergoing some kind of forced exile connected with his preaching of the Gospel. He is told by a voice to write down what he sees and send it around to seven churches in western Asia Minor. In 1:12-17a John describes what he saw: the glorious figure of the risen Christ. The description of him as "one like the Son of Man" is ambiguous. On the one hand he looks like a human being, but he is more than that. On the other hand he looks like the Son of Man, that is, the person of Jesus who suffered a painful and shameful death and yet was raised from the dead to eternal glory. All the biblical images used to describe him contribute to the picture of his dazzling glory. His holding the seven stars (the known planets?) in his right hand underscores his sovereignty over creation, and the sharp two-edged sword coming from his mouth indicates the power of his word.

In 1:17b-19 John describes what he heard: the voice of the one like the Son of Man identifying himself as "the first and the last"—titles appropriate to a divine being. The voice also claims "I was dead, and see, I am alive forever and ever," terms that fit the person of Jesus. He also claims now to have authority over death itself: "I have the keys of Death and of Hades." In 1:19 the risen Christ gives John a commission to write down what he will see concerning the present ("what is") and the future ("what is to take place after this"). A parenthetical comment in 1:20 identifies the seven stars as the (guardian) angels of the seven churches to be addressed in 2:1–3:22, and the seven lampstands as the seven churches.

Reasons for Hope: John is in exile on Patmos, far from the seven churches. Christians in those churches are undergoing internal divisions as well as external threats from the local Roman imperial officials and the local Jewish communities. Both the writer and those addressed stand in need of hope and encouragement in their sufferings. The source of their hope is the risen Christ. He is now a glorious figure, one who has conquered death and will live forever. To suffering and discouraged Christians the risen Christ offers perspective and consolation. Those who remain faithful to Christ will overcome all their tribulations and will be rewarded with eternal life in the New Jerusalem. From start to finish the book of Revelation is a document of hope for God's faithful servants in Christ.

2. TREE OF LIFE (REVELATION 2:1-7)

"To everyone who conquers,
I will give permission to eat from the tree of life
that is in the paradise of God." (Rev 2:7b)

Trees are a welcome sight. They are signs of life and growth. They give shade from the sun and shelter from the rain. Those who live in areas where the leaves die and fall from the trees, only to come to life again in the spring and grow even more abundantly, find in such trees a natural symbol of death and resurrection.

Background: The "tree of life" appears first in the second account of creation in Gen 2:4a-25. We are told in 2:8-9 that God planted a garden for Adam in Eden and placed in it two trees: "the tree of life also in the midst of the garden, and the tree of the knowledge of good and evil" (2:9). Then, after the disobedience of Adam and Eve in eating from the second tree, God feels obliged to make sure that Adam does not "reach out his hand and take also from the tree of life, and eat, and live forever" (2:22). The tree of life is a symbol of eternal life, and Adam forfeited that through his sin (3:19). Therefore God drove Adam out from the garden and placed the cherubim and a flaming sword "to guard the way to the tree of life" (3:24).

John: Revelation 2:1–3:22 contains seven "letters" or messages from the risen Christ to the "angels" of the following churches in western Asia Minor: Ephesus, Smyrna, Pergamum, Thyatira, Sardis, Philadelphia, and Laodicea. The messages begin with details used in John's description of the risen Lord in 1:12-20. The body of each letter offers praise and/or blame for the church. Then there is a call to listen and a promise to those who "overcome."

The message to the church at Ephesus (2:1-7) can serve to illustrate the pattern. First John is told to write to the "angel" of the church there. Next the speaker identifies himself as the risen Christ who holds the seven stars and walks among the seven golden lampstands (2:1; see 1:12, 16, 20). Then the church at Ephesus is praised for its patient endurance and resistance to false teachers (2:2-3, 6) and is criticized for its spiritual tepidity (2:4-5). Finally there is a call to hear (2:7a) and a promise that those who overcome will "eat from the tree of life that is in the paradise of God" (2:7b).

Most readers of Revelation today focus on the problems confronting the seven churches and the reasons why they are praised. These short reports provide precious glimpses into early Christian life and remind us that some of the problems facing the church today are not so different or new. It is important, however, not to overlook the word of hope with which each letter concludes.

These words of hope, or promises, are made to those who "conquer" or "overcome," that is, to those Christians who remain faithful to their calling in the face of persecution from outside the Christian community and turmoil and confusion from within the community. These promises inspired the famous song "We Shall Overcome," the anthem of hope for the civil rights movement in the United States in the 1960s.

The promise to "eat from the tree of life that is in the paradise of God" (2:7b) amounts to the reversal of Adam's fate in being driven out of the Garden of Eden. Whereas Adam was banished from paradise and sentenced to die, and so was unable to eat from the tree of life, those who overcome in their following of Christ will be invited into paradise and eat from the tree of life and so "live forever" (compare Gen 3:22).

The promises concluding the remaining six letters develop the theme of hope for eternal life as the reward for fidelity in the present with various images of hope: the crown of life (2:10), the hidden manna and the white stone (2:17), sharing in the Messiah's rule (2:27-28), the white robe and inclusion in the book of life (3:5), being a pillar in God's temple (3:12), and sitting with Christ and the Father on their throne (3:23).

Reasons for Hope: The ultimate hope of Christians is eternal life with Christ and his Father. The image of the tree of life appears at the beginning of the Christian Bible (Gen 2:9; 3:22-24) and at its end (Rev 22:2, 19). Whereas Adam lost his (and our) chance to eat from the tree of life in the Garden of Eden, those who remain faithful to their Christian faith in times of trial are promised the opportunity to eat from this tree and to enjoy eternal life. The fate of Adam has been reversed through Christ, and the hope of immortality has been made available to all.

3. SLAIN LAMB (REVELATION 5:6-14)

"Then I saw between the throne and four living creatures and among
the elders a Lamb standing as if it had been slaughtered,
having seven horns and seven eyes, which are the seven spirits
of God sent out into all the earth." (Rev 5:6)

A lamb is a young sheep, usually under one year old. Throughout history lambs have often been butchered for food, raised to adulthood for their wool, or offered in animal sacrifices to various deities. When applied to humans, the image of the lamb is used to characterize a person's innocence, gentleness, meekness, or physical weakness.

Background: In ancient Israelite worship lambs were frequently offered in various sacrifices as part of the Jerusalem Temple system of worship, especially in making expiation or atonement. To give back to God a choice lamb was regarded as a special offering. The lamb was an important element in the celebration of the first Passover in Egypt. In Exodus 12 the Lord instructs Moses that each household should have a lamb to eat, and that its blood is to be put on the doorposts and lintel of the house. The reason is given in Exod 12:13: "The blood shall be a sign for you on the house where you live; when I see the blood, I will pass over you." At later celebrations of Passover the lambs were first sacrificed at the Temple and then eaten in private homes.

In John's gospel (1:29, 36) John the Baptist hails Jesus as "the Lamb of God who takes away the sin of the world." According to Johannine chronology Jesus died at the exact time when the Passover lambs were being sacrificed in the Temple, on the afternoon before the first evening of Passover. In Isa 53:7 (see also Jer 11:19) the Servant of God is described as "like a lamb that is led to the slaughter, and like a sheep that before its shearers is silent." And in Acts 8:32-35 these words of the prophet are interpreted for the Ethiopian eunuch by Philip the evangelist as applying to and fulfilled in Jesus the Servant of God.

John: Taking up various threads from the Old Testament and transforming them, John in Rev 5:6 (see also 5:12 and 13:8) portrays the heavenly Christ as the Slain Lamb ("a lamb standing as if it had been slaughtered"). Thus he identifies the risen Lord as the one who underwent a sacrificial death "for our sins," brought to fulfillment the promise of Passover (freedom from slavery) in the paschal mystery of his death and resurrection, and now reigns as the Messiah ("the Lion of the tribe of Judah, the Root of David") and the Servant of the Lord despite (or rather, because of) his shameful death on the cross.

The setting for the revelation of the risen Christ as the Slain Lamb is the heavenly court. Summoned to heaven ("come up here"), John is promised in 4:1 that he will see what will take place in the future. The heaven he enters is like what people of his time imagined the Roman imperial throne room to be. The one seated on the throne is God pictured in great brilliance (4:2-3), surrounded by twenty-four (12 x 2) elders seated on twenty-four thrones (4:4) and the four "living creatures" singing the praises of God (4:6b-11). The scene combines the language of Ezekiel 1 and Isaiah 6. The heavenly chorus praises God as "our

Lord and God"—very likely a deliberate allusion to the claims that the Roman emperor Domitian was "Lord and God" *(dominus et deus)*.

The mood is broken in 5:1-5 by John's catching sight of a scroll with seven seals in the hand of the one seated on the throne and by the voice of an angel who asks: "Who is worthy to open the scroll and break its seals?" Unless the seals are broken and the scroll is opened, the future cannot come about and John cannot bear witness to what must take place. His disappointment and frustration are assuaged when he learns from one of the elders that the Messiah who has "conquered" (overcome death) can open the scroll.

In a startling change of images in 5:6 the Lion of Judah turns into the Slain Lamb. This shift highlights the Christian redefinition of "Messiah" from a Jewish military-political leader (see Psalms of Solomon 17) into Jesus the Suffering Servant of Isaiah 53, whose death has expiatory value "for us" and "for our sins." The Lamb is said to have "seven horns" and "seven eyes." The horn is a symbol of strength and the eye is a symbol of knowledge, and seven is the "perfect" number that occurs frequently in Revelation. The paradox is that the Slain Lamb is not weak and innocent, but rather is omnipotent and omniscient.

In a scene reminiscent of Daniel 7, where the Ancient One hands on power to one "like a son of man" (Michael?), the Slain Lamb in 5:7 receives the scroll from the one seated on the throne. In response (5:8-10) the twenty-four elders sing a "new song" (befitting a new moment in God's saving plan) and proclaim the Lamb to be worthy of this honor because in his being slaughtered he has "ransomed for God" by his blood the saints from all nations and made them into a "kingdom and priests serving our God." In 5:11-14 the angels join in the chorus and proclaim the Slain Lamb (5:12) to be worthy of all honor, even to the point of sharing glory with the one seated on the throne.

Reasons for Hope: The risen Christ portrayed as the Lamb that was slaughtered is the basis of Christian hope. The image of the Slain Lamb captures the central paradox of Christian faith. Jesus the Messiah (the Lion of Judah, the Root of David) fulfilled his task of bringing humankind into right relationship with God through his becoming the Slain Lamb (the paschal mystery). This gentle and humble teacher underwent a cruel death for us, and thus gave us all a reason for hope. His suffering is the ground of our hope. As Isa 53:5 says about the Servant of God, the one "like a lamb that is led to the slaughter" (53:7): "upon him was the punishment that made us whole, and by his bruises we were healed."

4. FOUR HORSEMEN (REVELATION 6:1-8)

"I looked, and there was a white horse! Its rider had a bow; a crown
was given to him, and he came out conquering and to conquer."
(Rev 6:2)

The horse is among the most powerful, graceful, and beautiful animals in creation. In biblical times horses belonged mainly to kings and wealthy persons, since they were expensive to keep fed and groomed. Poor people made do with donkeys and mules.

Background: According to 1 Kings 4:26, Solomon had forty thousand stalls of horses for his chariots and twelve thousand horsemen. Horses were used in battle, as the magnificent description of the horse in Job 39:19-25 shows: "Do you give the horse its might? . . . It paws violently, exults mightily; it goes out to meet the weapons."

The most pertinent biblical background, however, for Rev 6:1-8 appears in the book of Zechariah. The first eight chapters of that work concern efforts at rebuilding the Jerusalem Temple around 520 B.C.E., shortly after Israel's return from exile in Babylon. The first vision in the book (1:7-17) describes men riding on different-colored (red, sorrel, and white) horses. The angelic interpreter tells the prophet that the horsemen have patrolled the earth and determined that now is the time to rebuild the

Temple. The eighth and final vision (6:1-8) features four chariots with different-colored (red, black, white, and dappled gray) horses. They too have patrolled the earth in all directions and have found that Persia (Judea was then part of the Persian empire) is at peace. In Zechariah the horsemen and their horses play a positive role in encouraging the sixth-century Judean community to get to work on rebuilding the Temple.

John: The image of the four horsemen with their different-colored (white, red, black, and pale green) horses in Rev 6:1-8 clearly depends on and evokes Zech 1:7-17 and 6:1-8. But as always John changes things, most notably the character of the horsemen's mission. Whereas in Zechariah the horsemen and their horses play a positive and constructive role in encouraging the rebuilding of the Jerusalem Temple, in Rev 6:1-8 their works appear to be destructive against the enemies of God's people. However, even in their apparent destructiveness the four horsemen serve as images of hope for John and his beleaguered readers.

The four horsemen are part of the first of several series of seven members (septets) that give structure to Revelation: the seven seals, the seven trumpets, the seven bowls, and the seven last things. Whether the septets make the same point repeatedly (recapitulation) or show a linear progress has long been debated.

The opening of the first two seals in 6:2-3 brings on warfare. The first horseman (6:2) rides a white horse and carries a bow. The only archers (mounted riders shooting arrows) in battle in the first century were Parthians (or Persians). These fierce fighters terrified the Romans because the Parthians occupied the eastern borders of the Roman empire and made incursions into Roman territory. If any political power was going to defeat Rome, it would be Parthia. The crown the first rider wears is a symbol of victory, and he is described as a victor in battle: "he came out conquering and to conquer." The second horseman (6:3) on the red horse contributes further to the theme of military victory: "he was given a great sword."

The opening of the third seal (6:5-6) brings with it famine. The rider on the black horse has scales in his hand, and a voice proclaims that a quart of wheat and three quarts of barley will cost a whole day's wages. The opening of the fourth seal (6:7-8) brings pestilence and death. The rider on the pale green horse is named Death and is accompanied by "Hades" (the abode of the dead). The mission of the four horsemen is summarized in 6:8 as bringing death with "sword, famine, and pestilence, and by the wild animals of the earth."

Reasons for Hope: How could these four horsemen be images of hope? They could be such at least to John's first readers. The targets of the four horsemen were the sinful people of the Roman empire, who were persecuting the Christians of western Asia Minor. In the midst of their trials and tribulations these scenes were signs of hope for the eventual vindication of John's readers. They also pointed toward the second coming of Christ as the divine warrior who will ride a white horse (19:11) and his heavenly armies who will wear white linen and ride white horses (19:14). These forces will defeat the kings of the earth and prepare the way for the New Jerusalem. The four horsemen of Rev 6:1-8 anticipate the second coming of Christ and the fullness of God's reign. In that way they were and are images of hope.

5. WHITE ROBES (REVELATION 7:9-17)

"'Who are these, robed in white, and where have they come from?' . . . 'These are they who have come out of the great ordeal; they have washed their robes and made them white in the blood of the Lamb.'" (Rev 7:13-14)

The color white is often a symbol of (ritual, moral, sexual) purity and of victory. In Christian practice those who have been baptized wear a white garment. During the Christmas and Easter seasons priests wear white vestments at Mass. In the rite of Christian burial a white cloth is placed over the casket, and the priest wears white vestments.

Background: Revelation 7 contains several images of hope pertaining to the people of God that have rich biblical backgrounds. The "seal" (see Ezek 9:4, 6) reflects the idea that the 144,000 belong to God; they are now God's possession. The number 144,000 is a multiple of twelve, an allusion to the twelve tribes that constituted ancient Israel as God's people. The fact that each tribe is named and consists of twelve thousand members reinforces that notion. The white robes worn by the "great multitude" evoke the biblical connotations of innocence and victory. And palm branches were used in connection with the Jewish feast of Tabernacles and were part of the rededication of the Jerusalem Temple in the second century B.C.E. (see 1 Macc 13:51) and the celebration accompanying Jesus' entrance into Jerusalem on "Palm Sunday" (John 12:13). The "blood" of the Lamb is reminiscent of the blood associated with the first Passover (Exodus 12).

John: In each of the septets in Revelation there is an interlude between the sixth and seventh members of the series. The interlude in Revelation 7 provides the images of the 144,000 "sealed out of every tribe of the people of Israel" (7:1-8) and of the "great multitude" who have come out of the "great ordeal" (7:9-17).

The most startling image comes in the description of the great multitude. They are robed in white (7:13). The image suggests that these people remained faithful during the great tribulation or ordeal. They have preserved their moral innocence or purity by refusing to worship the emperor and the goddess Roma. There may also be sexual overtones here, since in the Old Testament idolatry or the worship of false gods is often described in terms of adultery or prostitution. In this sense they are victors or conquerors, and their victory is symbolized with white robes and palm branches.

What is truly startling is the reason why their robes are white: "they have washed their robes and made them white in the blood of the Lamb" (7:14). Who would wash a robe in blood and expect it to come out white? The imagery suggests that the

great multitude consists of Christian martyrs. They have suffered death on account of their fidelity to Jesus Christ. Their
moral innocence and victory over death are due to their participation in the paschal mystery of Jesus' life, death, and resurrection. The imagery of white robes washed in the blood of the
Lamb links their triumph to the triumph of Jesus over death in
his Passion, death, and resurrection.

Revelation contains what appear to be many fragments of
hymns interspersed throughout the text. These "hymns" are
pastiches made up of Old Testament phrases interpreted in
light of the paschal mystery. Two such fragments in 7:9-17 give
special prominence to Christ as the Lamb of God: "Salvation
belongs to our God who is seated on the throne, and to the
Lamb" (7:10), and "the Lamb at the center of the throne will be
their shepherd" (7:17). Just as the blood of the Lamb saved Israel at the first Passover (Exod 12:13), so faithful Christians will
be saved by the blood of Christ the Lamb of God.

Reasons for Hope: Revelation was first written for Christians who were suffering on account of their fidelity to the Gospel. John promises that their fidelity even to the point of death
will be respected and rewarded by God and the Lamb. Their
moral purity and victory symbolized by their white robes are
related to the paschal mystery of Jesus' life, death, and resurrection. Their hope (and the hope of all Christians) resides in the
blood of the Lamb. His blood has the power to produce clean
white robes for God's faithful servants.

6. SCROLL (REVELATION 10:8-11)

*"So I took the little scroll from the hand of the angel and ate it; it was
sweet as honey in my mouth, but when I had eaten it, my stomach
was made bitter."* (Rev 10:10)

In biblical times important literary works and letters were
written down on sheets of papyrus or leather (animal skin) that
were sewn together and then wound around a stick or pole to

form a scroll. To read the text one unrolled the scroll, section by section. The Isaiah scroll from Qumran, one of the Dead Sea scrolls, is about twenty-four feet long and contains the whole biblical book. As in Revelation 5, a scroll containing an important or official letter was often bound up by seals. The seals guaranteed the security and confidentiality of the communication and identified the source of the letter by name or symbol. While Jews continued to use scrolls, early Christians quickly adopted the codex (like our books) as their preferred vehicle of preserving their sacred books and other documents.

Background: According to Jeremiah 36 the prophet orders his secretary Baruch to take a scroll and write down his prophecies about impending doom for Judah. When that scroll was read in the court of King Jehoiakim, the king cut it up and threw it into the fire. Jeremiah then dictated another scroll, adding to the threats against Judah and its king.

The real biblical prototype for Rev 10:8-11, however, is Ezek 2:8–3:2. Here God addresses Ezekiel in the usual way as "mortal" (literally, "son of man/Adam") and tells him not to be rebellious as his people have been. He orders Ezekiel to open his mouth and eat what he gives him. What God gives Ezekiel is a written scroll with "words of lamentation and mourning and woe" (2:10). When Ezekiel eats the scroll he reports that "in my mouth it was as sweet as honey" (3:3). It was sweet because it contained the word of God that the prophet was to proclaim to the people of Israel and that was to come to fulfillment.

John: In Rev 10:8-11 John is told by a heavenly voice to eat a little scroll, much as Ezekiel did. But as usual there is a difference from the biblical model. Here John is told that the scroll "will be bitter to your stomach but sweet as honey in your mouth." The change takes account of the sadness associated with the prophet's mission. The words on the scroll are sweet because they are God's words, but bitter because they bring with them much suffering as well as hostility to the prophet himself as their bearer. Moreover, John's prophetic mission concerns not merely Israel as Ezekiel's mission does, but "many peoples and nations and languages and kings." John is a prophet to and for the whole world.

The scene with John eating the scroll is part of the interlude in the series of seven trumpets (8:6–11:19). The trumpet blasts serve as warnings about the coming of God's judgment. They describe the future displays of God's wrath against idolaters and other sinners (see 9:20-21) that issue in the ultimate display of divine justice in the full coming of God's reign.

The first four trumpet blasts (8:6-13) are loosely based on the plagues sent upon Egypt before the Exodus in Moses' time. The fifth trumpet blast (9:1-12) signals the appearance of huge locusts arising out of the bottomless pit, while the sixth (9:13-21) brings with it a huge army with powerful and terrifying horses described in a way to increase the Romans' fear of the Parthians.

The long interlude (10:1–11:14) features the prophetic commissioning of John (10:1-11) and the narrative about the martyrdom and resurrection of the "two witnesses" (11:1-14). The seventh trumpet blast (11:15-19) celebrates the eternal kingship of "our Lord and his Messiah," while the twenty-four elders proclaim that the time for divine judgment has arrived. The series ends with something like the theophany of Exodus 19, though on a much grander scale.

Reasons for Hope: In the interlude between the sixth and seventh trumpet blasts John is commissioned to proclaim God's judgment on the world. As a prophet he speaks the words given him by God. Because they are God's words, the prophet's task is sweet as honey. But because these words will also evoke suffering and hostility against God's prophet, the prophet's task is bitter. Nevertheless, John the prophet recognizes that his task is ultimately one of bringing hope to God's faithful. However difficult that task may be, John's calling as God's prophet demands that he proclaim both the best and the most bitter aspects of God's words.

7. WOMAN (REVELATION 12:1-18)

"A great portent appeared in heaven: a woman clothed with the sun, with the moon under her feet, and on her head a crown of twelve stars." (Rev 12:1)

These days it is difficult to make generalizations about women. However, it seems safe enough to say that many women bear children, nurture and educate them, and protect them from harm. Moreover, many women live in some danger of attack and often need to find ways to escape from violence being done to them and their children. These general characteristics certainly fit the woman described in Revelation 12.

Background: Most Christians, especially Catholics, instinctively identify the woman described in Revelation 12 as Mary, the mother of Jesus. Statues of Mary in practically every Catholic church in the world are influenced by the description presented above from Rev 12:1. And the identification is certainly not wrong. The woman is the mother of the Messiah. However, John invites us to view this woman in an even larger context.

Part of this larger context comes from the first pages of the Old Testament. While the sin of the first Eve resulted in enmity between her offspring and that of the serpent (Gen 3:15), the serpent will be struck down in connection with the Messiah's birth and life (12:7-9). Just as another effect of Eve's sin was pain in childbirth for women (Gen 3:16), so the new Eve cries out "in birthpangs, in the agony of giving birth" (12:2). And just as Eve was declared "the mother of all living" in this age/world (Gen 3:20), so the woman of Revelation 12 will be the mother of all those who live in the new age/world inaugurated by Jesus the Messiah.

Other elements in the background of Revelation 12 include the personification of Israel in the Old Testament as "daughter Zion" (Zeph 3:14), as well as the Jewish apocalyptic myth of the cosmic battle between the archangel Michael and Satan (see 1 Enoch 6–16 and the Qumran War Scroll). Also in the background

may be the ancient Near Eastern mythology associated with the
Great Mother goddess who was venerated for many centuries
especially in western Asia Minor—the area addressed in Revelation. There may also be echoes of the Greek myth surrounding the birth of the god Apollo. According to this myth Leto,
who conceived Apollo by Zeus, was pursued by Python (meaning "Serpent"). The latter was in turn slain by Apollo after his
birth.

John: Revelation 12 represents the approximate center of the
book and marks an important point in its development. It consists of three scenes: the woman and the dragon (vv. 1-6), Michael
and the dragon (vv. 7-12), and the woman and the dragon (vv.
13-18). In these scenes the child is Jesus the Messiah, the dragon
is Satan, and the woman is at once the people of God, the mother
of the Messiah, and the church. With these scenes John is explain-
ing what Jesus' death and resurrection mean, why the seven
churches are being persecuted, and how long it will last.

In the first scene (12:1-6) the woman about to give birth to
her child is menaced by a "great red dragon," which is an ancient Near Eastern image for the forces hostile to God. He wants
to destroy the child (the Messiah) at the moment of his birth.
The identity of the child is established by an allusion to the
"messianic" Ps 2:9: "who is to rule all the nations with a rod of
iron." The child escapes from the dragon by being "snatched
away and taken to God and to his throne" (12:5), which is a reference to Jesus' resurrection and ascension. The woman (the
church) meanwhile flees to the wilderness, to a safe place, where
she is to remain for 1,260 days, a figure taken from Daniel to describe the relatively short time of three and a half years.

In the second scene (12:7-12) there is a battle in heaven in
which Michael and his angels defeat the dragon and his angels.
The dragon is identified as "the ancient serpent, which is called
the Devil and Satan, the deceiver of the whole world" (12:9).
This cosmic battle means that the war against evil has been
won, even though the dragon will be allowed to carry on the

struggle on earth for a while. The heavenly voice proclaims that the war was won "by the blood of the Lamb" (12:11).

In the third scene (12:13-18) the dragon pursues the woman on earth. But she is able to escape, and even the earth and other forces of nature intervene on her behalf. Nevertheless, the dragon seeks to carry on the battle on earth against the woman and her child, who are defined as "those who keep the commandments of God and hold the testimony of Jesus" (12:17).

Reasons for Hope: John's message was that the churches of Asia Minor were being persecuted because Satan is on the loose, but this is only temporary. The woman of Revelation 12 is a sign of hope. She is the New Eve, God's people personified, the mother of the Messiah, and the church all in one. The polyvalent character of this figure helps us to understand better why Mary, the mother of Jesus, has been and is a sign of hope for so many people. Revelation 12 reminds us that the cosmic war against evil has already been won by "the blood of the Lamb," even though the struggle goes on. The attacks against the woman and her children are real and painful and frightening. But the enemies of the woman will not prevail in the end.

8. BEASTS (REVELATION 13:1–14:20)

"And I saw a beast rising out of the sea, having ten horns and seven heads; and on its horns were ten diadems, and on its heads were blasphemous names." (Rev 13:1)

One of the customary features of horror films designed to scare their audiences is the appearance of huge and grotesque beasts. These animals generally look something like the animals with which we are familiar, but they also tend to incorporate features from other different and even more frightening animals, put together in bizarre ways to add to the terror. This is not a new device. It was a staple of Jewish apocalyptic.

Background: Besides the great red dragon, Revelation 13 places before us "a beast rising out of the sea" (the Mediterranean) and "another beast that rose out of the earth" (western Asia Minor). There may be some connection here with the sea monsters and cattle of Gen 1:21 and 1:25, respectively, who in later Jewish writings are given the names Leviathan and Behemoth. For descriptions of these beasts in terms of the crocodile and the water buffalo, respectively, see Job 40:15–41:34.

A more obvious background for Revelation 13 appears in Dan 7:1-7. In Daniel's dream vision he sees four great beasts coming up out of the sea: the first is like a lion, the second is like a bear, the third is like a leopard, and the fourth has iron teeth and ten horns. In the context of Daniel the four beasts represent the four empires that ruled over Judea from the Babylonian exile (587 B.C.E.) to the writer's own time (165 B.C.E.): the Babylonians, the Medes, the Persians, and the Greeks (from Alexander the Great to Antiochus IV Epiphanes). The last beast is Alexander the Great.

John: In Revelation 13 the dragon and the two beasts represent, respectively, Satan, the Roman emperor, and the local political and/or religious official who was promoting the cults of the emperor and of the goddess Roma. Together they form a kind of unholy trinity fighting against the Christian churches. The two beasts are empowered by the dragon to do his bidding on earth.

The beast from the sea (13:1-10) has features from the beasts of Daniel 7. It displays symbols of authority ("on its horns were ten diadems"), and on its head are blasphemous names ("Lord and God"). Its head that received a death blow but healed probably refers to the emperor Nero's suicide in 68 C.E., from which many (wrongly) thought he had recovered (see 13:12). In worshiping this beast people were in fact worshiping the dragon (Satan). What was at issue for Christians like John was the question: Who really is Lord and God—the emperor Domitian, or the risen Jesus?

The beast from the land (13:11-18) is described as having two horns like a lamb (see Daniel 8) and speaking like a dragon. He was the local official who was promoting the emperor cult and so was in the service of the first beast and the dragon. He put on theatrical displays in order to attract and deceive the people. He demanded that all the people be "sealed" with the emperor's seal and use coins with the emperor's image on them in order to show that they belonged to the emperor. Compare Rev 7:4 and 14:1, where the 144,000 are marked with God's seal. The number of the first beast (the emperor) is 666. This is generally interpreted as the sum of the numerical equivalents of the Hebrew letters for "Nero Caesar," the Roman emperor famous for his persecution of Christians: N (= 50), R (= 200), W (= 6), N (= 50), Q (= 100), S (= 60), and R (= 200).

While the unholy trinity of the dragon and the two beasts represents a formidable enemy, it will be no match for the Lamb and his 144,000 companions (14:1-5). The 144,000 are called "virgins" because they have refused to participate in the idolatrous worship being promoted by the unholy trinity. The three angels (14:6-13) issue proclamations of judgment on the opponents of God's people, and that judgment is portrayed in 14:14-20 with two "harvest" scenes (of grain and grapes).

Reasons for Hope: The central portion of Revelation (chs. 12–14) acknowledges the reality of the early Christians' present sufferings brought on by Satan, the emperor, and the local official. Nevertheless, it stresses that the blood of the Lamb and God's promises provide sources for hope that the forces of evil can be overcome. It encourages Christians to stand up for their conviction that Jesus Christ (and not the emperor) is the real Lord and God. This is John's message of hope for Christian communities living under great pressures.

9. SEVEN PLAGUES (REVELATION 15–16)

"Then I saw another portent in heaven, great and amazing: seven
angels, with seven plagues, which are the last, for with them the
wrath of God is ended." (Rev 15:1)

For most people the word "plague" refers to some disease
that kills many persons. In the Middle Ages the bubonic plague
wiped out a large percentage of the inhabitants of Europe. Likewise, in the early twentieth century the "Spanish influenza"
epidemic spread to various parts of the world, leaving a huge
trail of death. However, the word "plague" (which comes from
the Greek *plēgē*) really has a more generic sense. In New Testament times *plēgē* could refer to a hard and sudden stroke with
some instrument, a wound caused by a blow, or an unexpected
calamity that caused severe distress.

Background: The biblical models for the seven last plagues
in Revelation 15–16 are the ten plagues visited upon ancient
Egypt before Israel's exodus. When Moses requested that the
Hebrews be released from slavery in Egypt, Pharaoh not only
refused but hardened his heart against them. As a way of con-
vincing Pharaoh to let Israel go, God sent ten plagues upon
Egypt. They are described in the book of Exodus as water
turned into blood (7:14-25), frogs (8:1-15), gnats (8:16-19), flies
(8:20-32), diseased livestock (9:1-7), boils (9:8-12), thunder and
hail (9:13-35), locusts (10:1-20), darkness (10:21-29), and the
death of the firstborn (12:29-32).

John: Just as the ancient Hebrews stood on the shores of
the Red Sea and celebrated God's saving action by singing the
Song of Moses (Exodus 15), so those who overcome the beast
will stand beside the "sea of glass" and sing the Song of Moses
and the Lamb that celebrates the justice and power of God (Rev
15:3-4). Then in the heavenly court (15:5-8) the seven angels
with the seven last plagues are given "seven golden bowls full
of the wrath of God."

The account of the seven last plagues in Revelation 16 uses many images from the ten plagues of Exodus. But it does not simply copy them or even preserve their order. The following list shows the influence of Exodus on Revelation: sores (Exod 9:10-11; Rev 16:2), seas and rivers becoming blood (Exod 7:17-21; Rev 16:3-4), darkness (Exod 10:22; Rev 16:10), drying up of the waters (Exod 14:21-22; Rev 16:12), frogs (Exod 8:3; Rev 16:13), and thunder and hail (Exod 9:24; Rev 16:18, 21). Even though the details and the order differ, the basic point of the two lists is clearly a message of hope to the effect that the God who led ancient Israel from slavery to freedom can do the same for Christians suffering oppression from the Roman empire.

The seven bowls of wrath in Revelation 16 are directed first of all at those "who had the mark of the beast and who worshiped its image" (16:2). They are punished because "they shed the blood of saints and prophets" (16:6). The sixth bowl gets poured out on the river Euphrates and dries it up, so that the armies on the other side (the Parthians) might cross over and terrorize the Romans (16:12). The enemies of Rome are abetted by foul and demonic spirits. Both sides assemble "at the place that in Hebrew is called Harmagedon" (16:16). That place-name is usually written in English as "Armageddon." It may refer to the "mountain of Megiddo" (*har Megiddo* in Hebrew), since Megiddo was a place of decisive battles in the Old Testament (Judg 5:19-20; 2 Kgs 23:29-30; 2 Chr 35:20-24). Or it may refer to Jerusalem as the site of the final battle (Zechariah 14). The account of the seventh plague (16:17-21) notes that "God remembered great Babylon and gave her the wine-cup of his wrath" (16:19). Babylon is a code-name for the Roman empire in Revelation (see also 1 Peter 5:13). Whatever bad things are said about Babylon in the Old Testament can, in John's view, now be said about the Roman empire.

Reasons for Hope: As with the series of seven seals and seven trumpets, the seven bowls of wrath prepare for the divine judgment against the enemies of God's people. The displays of divine wrath were intended to bring about repentance, though this is not always the result (see 6:16; 9:21; 16:21). The seven bowls are a sign of hope for the persecuted Christians being addressed by John. Just as the Exodus generation looked to God for "salvation" in Moses' time, so the persecuted Christians can and should look for salvation from God and the Lamb. But the object of their hope is eternal life in the reign of God, something far beyond the promised land the Exodus generation imagined.

10. HARLOT AND BRIDE (REVELATION 17:1–19:10)

"The woman was clothed in purple and scarlet, and adorned with gold and jewels and pearls, holding in her hand a golden cup full of abominations and the impurity of her fornication.". . . For the marriage of the Lamb has come, and his bride has made herself ready; to her it has been granted to be clothed with pure linen, bright and pure." (Rev 17:4; 19:7-8)

The word "harlot" refers to a woman who engages in sexual relations for pay. To attract customers she often dresses in flashy outfits, wears jewelry, and plies men with liquor. By contrast, the "bride" presents herself for marriage to her husband and dresses in white, the color of innocence and purity. Her clothing and demeanor are elegant, but also simple and modest.

Background: Prostitution has been described as the world's oldest profession. The most famous prostitute in the Old Testament is Rahab, the woman of Jericho who hides Joshua and Caleb and helps them escape so that they can carry on their mission to spy out the land of Canaan (Joshua 2). Other women described as prostitutes include Tamar (Genesis 38), the mother of Jephthah (Judg 11:1), and the two women whose dispute over a baby is settled by Solomon (1 Kgs 3:16). The images of fornication, adultery, and prostitution are often used negatively by the prophets to describe Israel's infidelity to its God and its fall into idolatry (see Hosea 1–4). By contrast, in the New Testament the church is portrayed positively as the bride of Christ (Eph 5:25-26).

John: In his prophecy about the fall of the Roman empire in 17:1–19:10, John contrasts two women: the prostitute who represents the Roman empire and the bride who represents the church. Whereas his pagan contemporaries were eager to worship the goddess Roma, it was John's contention that she was nothing but a harlot or whore. Whereas those same people looked down on Christians and tried to force them to worship the emperor and Roma, the church appears as the bride of the one who really is Lord and God.

John's vision of the harlot and the beast in 17:1-6 pictures Roma as a prostitute sitting on the beast (the emperor). She is described in garish terms and is named "Babylon," the code-name for Rome. She is said to be drunk "with the blood of the saints and the blood of the witnesses of Jesus" (17:6). The vision is accompanied by an interpretation in 17:7-18 that makes it clear that the vision concerns the Roman empire. Her seven heads are seven mountains, that is, the seven hills of Rome. The sketch of the Roman empire's history and the description of its war against the Lamb (who is "Lord of lords and King of kings") are concluded by a rather explicit statement: "The woman you saw is the great city that rules over the kings of the earth" (17:18).

The material between the contrasting descriptions of the two women celebrates proleptically (before the fact) the fall of the Roman empire. It does so in various literary forms: a lament (18:1-3), a prophecy (18:4-8), dirges from those who had profited from their dealings with Rome—kings, merchants, and sailors (18:9-20), and oracles of judgment (18:21-24). When John wrote Revelation, the Roman empire had not yet fallen. However, in John's view it was as good as already fallen, since the war against God's enemies had already been won by the blood of the Lamb.

The bride is described as part of the final heavenly chorus of "Hallelujahs" in 19:1-8. The song celebrates the triumph of the Lamb as part of a heavenly wedding celebration. The bride appears in simple and modest attire ("fine linen") and is described as "bright and pure."

Reasons for Hope: The sharp contrast between the two women, the harlot and the bride, makes the bride into a symbol of hope. In a parenthetical comment her garment of fine linen is identified as "the righteous deeds of the saints" (19:8). Even though the Roman empire remained in power when John wrote (and would continue for several more centuries), it was doomed in John's view because of the prophetic word against it. The hope John sought to encourage was rooted in the blood of the Lamb and the promises of God, not in military force or political power.

11. RIDER ON A WHITE HORSE (REVELATION 19:11-21)

"Then I saw heaven opened, and there was a white horse! Its rider is called Faithful and True, and in righteousness he judges and makes war." (Rev 19:11)

One of the standard features of the old "western" movies was the appearance of the man on the white horse. He often wore a white hat, just to be sure that we got the point. The prototype was the "Lone Ranger" with his horse "Silver." The rider on the white horse was very much a savior figure. He appeared at just the right time, when all else seemed hopeless, and managed to defeat the forces of evil and to leave the "good" people with renewed hope.

Background: Revelation's portrayal of the risen Christ as a divine warrior figure has deep roots in ancient Near Eastern mythology and in the Old Testament. The Song of Moses in Exodus 15, which is regarded by many as one of the oldest poems in the Bible, attributes the Exodus from Egypt to the power of the God of Israel as a warrior: "The Lord is a warrior; the Lord is his name" (Exod 15:3). Zechariah 9:9 celebrates either God or the Messiah (see Matt 21:5; John 12:15) as a warrior king: "Lo, your king comes to you; triumphant and victorious is he."

The book of Wisdom, composed in the first century B.C.E. in Alexandria, is concerned to show in chapters 10–19 how the figure of Wisdom personified was active and indeed instrumental in Israel's Exodus from Egypt. When describing the death of the Egyptian firstborn (the tenth plague) it attributes the carrying out of that punishment to Wisdom's action as a warrior: "your all powerful word leaped from heaven, from the royal throne, into the midst of a land that was doomed, a stern warrior carrying the sharp sword of your authentic command, and stood and filled all things with death, and touched heaven while standing on the earth" (18:15-16).

John: Thus far John has led us through three series of seven seals, trumpets, and bowls. At the end of each we get the impression that the full cycle of end-time events has been completed. He has also shown us, in chapter 12, the victory in the cosmic battle, and has prophesied the fall of Babylon (Rome) in 17:1–19:10 as if it had already happened. It is no wonder that many interpreters view Revelation from the perspective of recapitulation: that is, the same basic point is being repeated several times over in different forms and with different images. Nevertheless, John saw the need for one more decisive and climactic series of seven events: the *parousia* of the risen Christ (19:11-16), the first battle (19:17-21), the binding of Satan (20:1-3), the first resurrection (20:4-6), the final defeat of Satan (20:7-10), the last judgment (20:11-15), and the new heaven and the new earth (21:1-8).

In the first of these end-time events the risen Christ makes his appearance *(parousia)* as the divine warrior, the rider on the white horse. Two themes predominate in 19:11-16: the identity of the rider, and his clothing and weapons.

The identity of the rider is established by giving him a series of names and hinting that he has a secret name (19:12). He is first called "Faithful and True," in keeping with his own fidelity in suffering and the righteousness with which he lived. Then he is identified as the "Word of God," echoing both John 1:1 ("In the beginning was the Word") and Wis 18:15-16 ("your all powerful word"). The allusion to Ps 2:9 ("he will rule them with a rod of iron") reminds us that this warrior is the Messiah. And finally his secret name is revealed to be "King of kings and

Lord of lords," thus marking him as superior to the Roman emperor.

The divine warrior is clothed "in a robe dipped in blood," not the blood of his enemies but rather his own blood shed for us. His sharp sword is the word that comes forth from his mouth, and he judges and makes war in righteousness. This is no mere flesh-and-blood combat. Rather, it concerns the spiritual or heavenly realm, and so it demands the appropriate weaponry of righteousness and truth. The first battle in 19:17-21 involves the defeat of the two beasts, that is, the Roman emperor and the local official: "And the beast was captured, and with it the false prophet" (19:20). The defeat of Satan, the remaining member of the "unholy trinity," will come next.

Reasons for Hope: The man riding on the white horse is a savior figure. He appears at the decisive moment and initiates the final sequence of end-time events leading up to the full coming of God's reign. He is called Faithful and True, the Word of God, the Messiah, and the King of kings and Lord of lords. His weapons are righteousness and truth. He is the primary reason for Christian hope.

12. MILLENNIUM (REVELATION 20:4-6)

"I also saw the souls of those who had been beheaded for their testimony to Jesus and for the word of God. They had not worshiped the beast or its image and had not received its mark on their foreheads or their hands. They came to life and reigned with Christ a thousand years." (Rev 20:4)

In the year 2000 (or 2001) we celebrated the end of the second millennium and the beginning of the third millennium after the birth of Christ. That celebration had little or nothing to do with the millennium of Rev 20:4, though the popular media never seemed to grasp that point. The word "millennium" means a thousand years. It can refer to any thousand years. But the best known use of the word appears in Rev 20:4, which refers to the thousand-year reign of the faithful martyrs with the risen Christ on earth.

Background: The concept of the millennium is not found in the Old Testament. However, its roots can be discerned in descriptions of what will happen when the ideal king (the Messiah) arrives in such texts as Isa 11:1-9: "A shoot shall come out from the stump of Jesse . . . with righteousness he shall judge the poor and decide with equity for the meek of the earth . . . the wolf shall live with the lamb, the leopard shall lie down with the kid." The idea of a temporary messianic kingdom appears in the Jewish apocalypse known as 4 Ezra (2 Esdras) 7:26-30: "For my son the Messiah shall be revealed with those who are with him, and those who remain shall rejoice four hundred years" (7:28). The Messiah then dies at the end of the four hundred years.

John: In the final series of end-time events the description of the millennium (20:4-6) appears between the binding of Satan (20:1-3) and Satan's final defeat (20:7-10). The binding of Satan is to last a thousand years, and so it is a necessary presupposition for the millennium described in 20:4-6.

The millennium according to Rev 20:4-6 is for the Christian martyrs. These are the people who have remained faithful in the time of testing, to the point of being beheaded. Their witness concerned Jesus and the word of God. They refused to participate in the worship of the Roman emperor ("the beast or its image") and did not accept the mark of the beast (which signified belonging to the emperor).

The reward for these faithful witnesses is participation in the first resurrection. In the millennium they (and they alone) come to life and reign with Christ. The rest of the dead will come back to life only after the millennium (20:5). In their risen life the martyrs will be "priests of God and of Christ" (20:6). Christians are also called "priests" in Rev 1:6 and 5:10. Here the idea is that the resurrected martyrs will spend their thousand years chiefly in the worship of God and Christ. They will function in the new people of God in a way analogous to that of levitical priests in ancient Israel.

In the Catholic tradition the millennium of Rev 20:4-6 is generally understood in a symbolic or spiritual sense as referring to the saints reigning with Christ in victory. In some (generally very conservative) Protestant circles the millennium is interpreted as the literal reign of Christ on earth, though the requirement of martyrdom is usually ignored. The great debate in those circles concerns whether the second coming of Christ precedes the millennium (premillennialism) or follows it (postmillennialism). The concepts of the Antichrist (from 1 John) and rapture of the saints (from 1 Thess 4:16) are often combined with these positions to yield a roadmap for the future.

According to Rev 20:7-10, Satan will enjoy a temporary release, deceive many, and mount a campaign against the saints. However, his forces will be consumed by fire, and finally the dragon (Satan) will join the beast (the emperor) and the false prophet (the local official) in the lake of fire and suffer eternal torment. Thus the "unholy trinity" is defeated definitively.

Reasons for Hope: The millennium described in 20:4-6 is a very strange concept. However, when its details are not pushed too hard it can and should be a sign of hope for Christians. The martyrs who have died on account of their fidelity to God deserve the reward of resurrection and eternal life. This is also the fate to which all Christians, martyrs or not, can and should aspire. The hope of all Christians is to reign with the risen Christ.

13. LAST JUDGMENT (REVELATION 20:11-15)

"And I saw the dead, great and small, standing before the throne, and books were opened. Also another book was opened, the book of life. And the dead were judged according to their works, as recorded in the books." (Rev 20:12)

At the high school I attended many years ago there was a custom known as "the reading of marks." All three hundred or so members of a class assembled several times during a year in the school's auditorium and the principal read aloud the grades of each student, often with evaluative comments ("Good work" or "You need to study harder"). The rationale given for this practice was that "It's good preparation for the Last Judgment."

Background: In the early parts of the Old Testament it is assumed that in this life good and wise persons will be rewarded, and evil and foolish persons will be punished. This principle is called the law of retribution. However, the historical experience of Israel as a people or the individuals within it cast doubt on the general validity of this principle. The prophets looked increasingly to the historical "Day of the Lord" when God would set things right for his people. In some Jewish circles writers began to look beyond this life to life after death and to the general resurrection as the event when the righteous will be vindicated and the wicked will be punished (see Dan 12:1-3; 2 Maccabees 7; Wisdom 2–5; 4 Ezra 3–14).

In the New Testament and many contemporary Jewish writings the Last Judgment became a well-established article of faith. For example, the parables of the wheat among the weeds and of the fishing net in Matthew 13 assume that the Last Judgment will be part of the full coming of God's reign. Likewise, Matt 25:31-46 presents an elaborate scene of the Son of Man as the judge of "all the nations" and gives acts of kindness to "the least" as the criterion by which they will be judged. The Last Judgment is also a prominent theme in Paul's letters. For example, Paul insists that "on the day of wrath, when God's righteous judgment will be revealed . . . . he will repay according to each one's deeds" (Rom 2:5-6).

John: The sixth event in John's last scenario of end-time events is the Last Judgment (20:11-15). The one who presides is God: "a great white throne, and the one who sat on it." The resurrection of the dead is the necessary preparation for the Last Judgment, and all the dead ("great and small") stand before the throne.

The motif of the heavenly books is prominent in Jewish writings of the time. The idea is that these books contain the names of the righteous and of the wicked, as well as a record of their deeds. The "book of life" presumably contains the names of the righteous, those for whom the Last Judgment will mean vindication and reward. According to Rev 20:12 the criterion for the Last Judgment, as elsewhere in the New Testament and early Jewish writings, is one's deeds: "And the dead were judged according to their works, as recorded in the books."

The consequences of the Last Judgment are described in 20:13-15. Death (personified) and Hades (the abode of the dead) will give up all their dead, and will themselves be thrown into "the lake of fire" to join the unholy trinity of Satan and the two beasts (see 20:10). Those whose names do not appear in the book of life will also be thrown into the lake of fire. The "second death" they are to endure is most likely annihilation, that is, death after death. But those whose names are in the book of life will enjoy eternal life in the new heaven and new earth (21:1-4) where "death will be no more; mourning and crying and pain will be no more."

Reasons for Hope: For the wise and righteous the Last Judgment is very much an occasion for hope. Their sufferings on behalf of the Gospel will be recognized and rewarded. The Last Judgment will mean the definitive revelation of God as both omnipotent and just. But what about the others? God is the judge. We humans cannot put limits of the mercy of God. In fact, there are some reliable scholars who contend that there is evidence in Revelation for universal salvation on the basis of such texts as 5:13; 14:6-7; and 15:3-4. Even "the kings of the earth" will bring their glory into the New Jerusalem.

14. NEW JERUSALEM (REVELATION 21:9-27)

"And in the spirit he carried me away to a great, high mountain and showed me the holy city of Jerusalem coming down out of heaven from God." (Rev 21:10)

As a graduate student I lived in Jerusalem for one summer (1966) and then for a whole academic year (1968–69). I often took a walk that included the Holy Sepulchre (the church marking the place of Jesus' death and burial), the Dome of the Rock and Al-Aqsa Mosque (major Islamic shrines), and the Western Wall (remnants of the Jewish Second Temple complex), all in about forty-five minutes. Since then I have visited Jerusalem several times. I know the earthly Jerusalem well and love it. Nevertheless, the earthly Jerusalem is not perfect and never has been. It has pickpockets, pimps, and political opportunists. Tensions run high, and minor events can easily turn into international incidents. It can be a dangerous and disappointing place.

Background: In antiquity Jerusalem did not belong to any of the twelve tribes of Israel. That was one reason why King David made it his capital city. In the First Temple period (roughly 1000 to 587 b.c.e.) Jerusalem served as the political and religious center of Judah. Its Temple became the central shrine of the people of Israel. During the Babylonian exile (587 to 537 b.c.e.) the prophet Ezekiel laid out a verbal plan for a new and even more glorious Jerusalem in chapters 40–48 of the book that bears his name. Building the Second Temple began around 520 b.c.e. Whatever progress was made on the ground, there were still greater visions of what Jerusalem could and should be. Such imaginative visions have been found among the Dead Sea scrolls, especially in the Temple Scroll and in the New Jerusalem texts. Even with the destruction of the city and its temple in 70 c.e., hope for the new Jerusalem as the ideal and perfect city remained alive.

John: The vision of the New Jerusalem stands in line with Jewish hopes for the ideal city, one built not by human hands but by God. In a startling twist of images, an angel summons John: "Come, I will show you the bride, the wife of the Lamb." The bride is then transformed into the city. The holy city comes down from heaven. In other words, the builder of the city is God, not human workers.

John's description of the New Jerusalem incorporates elements from various biblical sources, but always in new combinations and in new contexts. Because it will have the glory of God, the New Jerusalem will shine with radiance and brilliance, clear as crystal (21:11). According to 21:12-14 it will have a great high wall all around it, with twelve gates, each bearing the name of one of the twelve tribes of Israel and also symbolizing the church (the twelve apostles of the Lamb).

The New Jerusalem will be huge in size (21:15-17). It will be a cube of 1,400 miles in all directions, and its wall will be 216 feet high. The wall will be made of jasper, and the city will be "pure gold, clear as glass" (21:18). The foundations of the city will be constructed of precious stones, the twelve gates will be made of gigantic pearls, and the city will be pure gold (21:19-21). While it may be hard to put all these images together, everything in the description of the New Jerusalem contributes to a sense of its great size and splendor. It will be more brilliant than any city made by humans.

Perhaps the most interesting features of John's vision of the New Jerusalem concern what is absent. First, there is no temple in the city, "for its temple is the Lord God the Almighty and the Lamb" (21:22). Temples and churches are built by humans as symbols or signs pointing to the presence of God among us. But in the New Jerusalem God and the Lamb (the risen Christ) will be present. There is no need for signs or symbols when the real thing ("Emmanuel") is truly and fully present.

Moreover, the New Jerusalem does not need light from the sun or the moon, since "the glory of God is its light, and its lamp is the Lamb" (21:23). The glory of God will illumine everything. The New Jerusalem will become the center of the world, attracting peoples and kings from all over. Its gates will never be shut, and everyone will be welcome (universal salvation?). There will be no moral or ritual impurity in the New Jerusalem (21:24-27).

Reasons for Hope: In the Lord's Prayer we ask that "your will be done on earth as it is in heaven" (Matt 6:10). John's vision of the New Jerusalem is an imaginative fulfillment of that petition. Both texts are expressions of hope for the full coming of God's kingdom. There is, however, no guarantee that John's vision will be fulfilled in an exactly literal way. Only time will tell. What is more important than the details is the recognition that it is God's kingdom to bring about and that God will do so when and how God sees fit.

15. RIVER OF LIFE (REVELATION 22:1-5)

"Then the angel showed me the river of the water of life, bright as crystal, flowing from the throne of God and of the Lamb, through the middle of the street of the city. On either side of the river is the tree of life with its twelve kinds of fruit, producing its fruit each month; and the leaves of the tree are for the healing of the nations."
(Rev 22:1-2)

The river of the water of life flows through the New Jerusalem. Most major cities throughout human history have been built near rivers. The rivers supply the people with water and also serve as channels for shipping and receiving food and other material goods. The school of theology where I have taught for many years is located a few blocks from the Charles River, which separates Cambridge and Boston, Massachusetts. The bridge that joins the two main campuses of Harvard University has an inscription bearing the text of Rev 22:1-2 quoted above. Every time I see that inscription I am filled with hope for the future and am challenged to work harder and do better for the good of others.

Background: Genesis 2 presents a description of the Garden of Eden in which "the tree of life" is a prominent feature (2:9). From Eden there flows out a river that divides and becomes four branches (2:10). In his vision of the New Jerusalem the prophet Ezekiel sees a river flowing from the temple (47:12). On its banks there will grow all kinds of trees, and "their fruit will be for food, and their leaves for healing." John's vision of the river of the water of life in Rev 22:1-2 puts together images from Gen 2:9-10 (the river of paradise and the tree of life) and Ezek 47:12 (the trees on the river banks supplying food and medicine). The images of water and trees contribute to the atmosphere of life in abundance that suffuses John's final vision of the New Jerusalem.

John: Life in the New Jerusalem is "heaven on earth." Just as in his inaugural vision in Revelation 4–5 John saw the whole heavenly court engaged in the worship of God and of the Lamb, so in the New Jerusalem the most prominent feature will be "the throne of God and of the Lamb, and his servants will worship him" (22:3). Those servants of God will proudly bear the name of God (not those of the emperor or Rome) on their foreheads. They will need no external source of light, "for the Lord God will be their light, and they will reign forever and ever" (22:5).

Like the book of Daniel, Revelation ends with a series of short sayings in 22:6-21. The major themes of these sayings are the trustworthiness of what has been said, the nearness of the time when these words will come to pass, and exhortations to keep these words and act upon them. Scattered among these final sayings are several statements about the greatness of Jesus that explain why he is the ground of Christian hope. In 22:13 the risen Christ identifies himself in this way: "I am the Alpha and the Omega, the first and the last, the beginning and the end." Alpha and Omega are the first and last letters in the Greek alphabet. These titles place the risen Christ on the same level as God the Father. The book of Revelation throughout has a very high estimation of Jesus and provides important evidence for early Christian belief in the divinity of Jesus.

In 22:16 the risen Jesus identifies himself as "the root and descendant of David" (the Messiah) and "the bright morning star" (the Risen One). Just as the planet Venus is the first object that is visible in the morning sky, so Jesus by his resurrection from the dead is the firstborn from the dead and the ground of all our hope in resurrection.

In 22:20 there is the plea "Come, Lord Jesus!" This is a prayer for the second coming of Christ and the fullness of God's reign, one of the elements of Christian faith. Its Aramaic form appears in 1 Cor 16:22 as "Maranatha!" The whole of the book of Revelation is summarized in the prayer "Come, Lord Jesus!"

Reasons for Hope: The basis of Christian hope is the life, death, and resurrection of Jesus. The object of Christian hope is fullness of life in the kingdom of God. The horizon of Christian life and hope is eternal life with God and the Lamb in the New Jerusalem. This is the New Testament theology of hope in a nutshell.

A Concluding Word of Hope

"May the God of hope fill you with all joy and peace in believing,
so that you may abound in hope by the power of the Holy Spirit."
(Rom 15:13)

What emerges from all these essays is the recognition that the New Testament (and the entire Bible) is a book of Christian hope. It begins with the hope that the child Jesus will be "Emmanuel" and ends with the plea "Come, Lord Jesus." The texts in the three very different books (Matthew, Romans, Revelation) treated in this volume underscore the ultimate Christian hopes (right relationship with God, eternal life with God, the fullness of God's reign) and thus provide the framework for exercising Christian hope in our everyday lives.

As Paul's prayer in Rom 15:13 indicates, Christian hope is in the final analysis a gift from "the God of hope," flows from faith and issues in joy and peace, and yields ever more abundant hope through the Holy Spirit. Nevertheless, Christian hope does not exempt us from the miseries, fears, and frustrations of everyday human existence, nor does it excuse us from our social responsibilities as family members and good citizens of the world. The Bible provides practical advice on all these matters in its Old Testament wisdom books (see especially

Proverbs, Sirach, Wisdom, and Ecclesiastes) and in its New Testament wisdom instructions (the Sermon on the Mount, Paul's "ethical advice," and the letter of James). The biblical texts about hope can and should infuse our everyday actions with respect for others, freedom, and optimism. As people of hope Christians ought to be signs of hope for those around them.

The images of hope spread through the New Testament remind us of our vocation to be people of hope, and can help us to make concrete and personal what may often seem largely transcendental ("beyond us") and eschatological. The use of images to convey their message of hope was the pedagogical strategy of Jesus, as well as of Matthew, Paul, and John, when they all tried to convey a vision of what has and will come to pass in the story of our salvation.

The texts discussed in this volume (and the many others that await your discovery) show us why Christians can be people of hope and remind us of our call to be signs of hope for others. A famous passage in 1 Peter 3:15-16 expresses beautifully the Christian vocation to be a sign of hope and how this calling should be carried out: "Always be ready to make your defense to anyone who demands from you an accounting for the hope that is in you; yet do it with gentleness and reverence."

FOR REFERENCE AND FURTHER STUDY

Aune, David E. *Revelation.* 3 vols. WBC 52a-c. Dallas: Word Books, 1997–98.

Bauckham, Richard, and Trevor Hart. *Hope Against Hope: Christian Eschatology at the Turn of the Millennium.* Grand Rapids: Eerdmans, 1999.

Byrne, Brendan. *Romans.* SP 6. Collegeville: Liturgical Press, 1996.

Davies, William D., and Dale C. Allison. *A Critical and Exegetical Commentary on the Gospel According to Saint Matthew.* ICC. Edinburgh: T & T Clark, 1988–97.

Desroche, Henri. *The Sociology of Hope*. London: Routledge & Kegan Paul, 1979.

Fitzmyer, Joseph A. *Romans*. AB 33. New York: Doubleday, 1993.

Harrington, Daniel J. *The Gospel of Matthew*. SP 1. Collegeville: Liturgical Press, 1991.

Harrington, Wilfrid J. *Revelation*. SP 16. Collegeville: Liturgical Press, 1993.

Moltmann, Jürgen. *The Coming of God: Christian Eschatology*. Minneapolis: Fortress, 1996.

_____. *In the End, the Beginning. The Life of Hope*. Minneapolis: Fortress, 2004.

_____. *Theology of Hope: On the Ground and the Implications of a Christian Eschatology*. New York: Harper & Row, 1967.

Pieper, Joseph. *On Hope*. San Francisco: Ignatius Press, 1986.

Volf, Miroslav, and William Katerberg, eds. *The Future of Hope: Christian Tradition amid Modernity and Postmodernity*. Grand Rapids: Eerdmans, 2004.

Index of Subjects

Abraham, 51–54
Adam, 56–59, 61–63

baptism, 9–10, 59–61
beasts, 99–101
boat, 18–21
body, 72–74
bride, 104–06
bridesmaids, 32–35

childbirth, 65–67
cry, 35–37

day, 74–77
Day of Atonement, 49–50
death, 59–61
divided self, 61–63
dragon, 98–99

Emmanuel, 4–6

father, 16–18
fishermen, 11–13

gospel, 42–46

harlot, 104–06
hope, vi–x
horse, 106–08
horsemen, 90–92

house, 77–79

judgment, 110–12
justification, 53–56

kingdom, 26–28

lamb, 87–90, 93–94
laments, 35–36
lectio divina, x
life, 59–61
light, 14–16
Lord's Prayer, 17–18

Magi, 7–8
meals, 21–23
millennium, 108–10

Nero, 100–01
New Jerusalem, 112–15
night, 74–77

olive tree, 70–72

parables, 27–28, 34–35
Parthians, 91
Peter, 11–13, 29–30
plagues, 102–04
priests, 109–10

remnant, 67–70
resurrection, 37–40
rider, 106–08
river of life, 115–17
robes, 92–94
rock, 28–30
Rome, 105

sacrifice, 49–51
salt, 14–16
salvation, 46–49
school, 24–25
scroll, 94–96
sinners, 22
Son of Man, 83–85

Spirit, 63–65, 67
star, 6–8
storm, 18–21

tax collectors, 22
tree of life, 85–87

vineyard, 30–32
virginal conception, 4–5

water, 8–10
wedding, 33–35
woman, 97–99

yoke, 23–25

INDEX OF ANCIENT TEXTS

Genesis
1	19
1–3	56–57, 59
1–11	52
1:2	10, 63
1:3	14, 75
1:21	100
1:25	100
2:4-25	85
2:9	87
2:9-10	115–16
2:17	62
3:15-16	97
3:16	65–66
3:19	85
3:20	97
3:22	86
3:22-24	87
3:24	85
6–8	68
12:1-3	52
15:4-6	53
17:10-27	53
18–19	68
22	52–53
22:2	10
38	5, 104

Exodus
7–12	102–03
12	87
12:13	88
15	102
15:3	106

19–24	53	7:14	4–5
25:31-40	83	9:2	12–13
40:12	9	10:22-23	68
		11:1-9	109
Leviticus		22:22	29
2:13	14	32:2	28
16	49–50	40–55	viii
16:4, 24	9	40:3	9
		40:9	44
Numbers		42:1	10
24:17	6–7	44:2	10
		52:7	44
Deuteronomy		53:5	90
7:13	70	53:7	88, 90
22:23-27	5	53:12	50
		60:6	44
Joshua		61:1	44, 64
2	5, 104		
		Jeremiah	
Judges		2:20	23
5:19-20	103	5:5	23
11:1	104	11:16	70–71
		11:19	88
2 Samuel		16:14-18	11–12
4:10	44	26	95
11–12	5	31:31-34	viii, 11
18:22	44		
18:25	44	*Ezekiel*	
22:2-3	28	1:1	10
		2:8–3:2	95
1 Kings		9:4	93
3:16	104	9:6	93
4:26	90	37	38
		40–48	113
2 Kings		43:24	14
23:29-30	103	47:12	115–16
Isaiah		*Hosea*	
1:9	68	1–4	104
2:5	14	2:23	69
5:1-7	31		
6:3	17–18		

6:6	23	7:13	83
14:6	71	8	101
		10:5-6	83
Micah		12:1-3	111
2:12	68	12:2-3	38
Zephaniah		*2 Chronicles*	
3:14	97	35:20-24	103
Zechariah		*4 Ezra*	
1:7-17	90–91	3–14	61–62, 111
4:1-2	83	7:26-30	109
6:1-8	91		
9:9	106	*1 Maccabees*	
14	103	13:51	93
Psalms		*2 Maccabees*	
2:7	10	7	38, 111
2:9	98, 107		
18:2	28	*Sirach*	
22	36–37	6:24-31	24
43:3	14	51:26-27	24
71:3	28		
72:10-11	7	*Wisdom*	
95:1	26	2–5	111
107:23-30	19–20	3:1	38
		3:4	38
Job		10–19	106–07
6:6	14	18:15-16	107
39:19-25	90		
40:15–41:34	100	*2 Baruch*	
		54:19	58
Proverbs			
9:1-6	21	*1 Enoch*	
		6–16	97–98
Ruth	5		
		Psalms of Solomon	
Daniel	viii	17	89
7	89		
7:1-7	100	*Community Rule (1QS)*	
7:9	83	3–4	54–55

124   *What Are We Hoping For?*

Matthew	1–3		16:21	39
1:1-25	4–6		16:22-33	30
1:18	4		17:22-23	39
1:19	5		18:18	29
1:20	4		20:1-16	30
1:23	4		20:17-19	39
2:1-12	6–8		21:5	106
2:2	6		21:33	30
3:2-3	9		21:33-46	30–32
3:9	68		22:22-33	38
3:11	9		23	3
3:13	8		23:8	32
3:13-17	8–10		24–25	34–35
4:17	26		24:8	66
4:18-22	11–13		25:1-13	32–35
4:19	11		25:2-3	32
5–7	14–15, 19		25:31-46	83, 111
5:3-12	14–15		26:69-75	30
5:13-14	14		27:25	3
5:13-16	14–16		27:45-54	35–37
5:45	viii		27:46	35
6:2-18	17		27:57-66	39
6:9	16		28:1-20	37–40
6:9-13	vii, 16–18, 80		28:6	37
6:10	1, 10, 114–15		28:19	8
6:13	66		28:20	6, 32
8–9	19			
8:18-27	18–21		*Mark*	
8:24	18		1:16-20	12
9:9	2		4:35-41	19–20
9:9-13	21–23		8:27-33	29
9:10	21		8:31	83
11:25-30	23–25		9:31	83
11:29	23		10:33-34	83
13:1-52	26–28, 111		12:1-12	31
13:31	26		13:8	66
14:28-31	29–30		15:34	36
16:13-20	28–30		*Luke*	
16:18	28		1:34	5

3:8	68
3:22	63
4:18	64
11:2-4	vii, 80
22:19	73

John

1:1	107
1:29	88
1:36	88
3:22	59
3:26	59
4:1	59
12:13	93
12:15	106
14–16	64
16:21	66

Acts

2	64
4:13	11
8:32-35	88
18:1-2	78

Romans	41–44
1:1-7	44–46
1:3-4	44, 47
1:16	46
1:16-17	46–49
1:18-32	48, 50
2:1–3:20	48, 50
2:5-6	111
3:21-26	49–51
3:25	49–50
4:1-25	51–54
4:18	51
5:1	54
5:1-11	54–56
5:12-21	56–59
5:15	56

6:1-11	59–61
6:4	59
7:7-25	61–64
7:24-25	61
8:1-17	63–65
8:14	63
8:18-39	65–67
8:22	65
9–11	68–69, 71–72
9:1-29	67–70
9:27	67
11:17-18	70
11:17-26	70–72
11:29	69
12:1	51
12:1-8	72–74
12:1–15:13	76
12:4-5	72
13:11-14	74–77
13:12	74
15:13	44, 117
16:1-16	77–79
16:3-4	77
16:21-23	77–79

1 Corinthians

11:24	73
12–14	73
16:22	117

2 Corinthians

10–13	61

Galatians

1:13-17	45, 61
2:20	62

Ephesians

2:19-22	77
5:21–6:9	78
5:25-26	104

Philippians		6:1-8	90–92
3:4-16	61	6:2	90
		7:4	101
Colossians		7:9-17	92–94
3:18–4:1	78	7:13-14	92
		8:6–11:19	96
1 Thessalonians		10:8-11	94–96
4:16	110	10:10	94
		12:1	97
1 Timothy		12:1-18	97–99
3:15	77	12:2	66
		13:1	99
Philemon		13:1–14:20	99–101
2	77	14:1	101
		14:6-7	112
Hebrews		15–16	102–04
3:1-6	77	15:1	102
10:9	51	15:3-4	112
13:15	51	17:1–19:10	104–06
		17:4	104
1 Peter		19:7-8	104
3:15-16	118	19:11	92, 106
5:13	103	19:11-21	106–08
		19:11–21:8	107
1 John	110	19:14	92
		20:4	108–09
2 John		20:4-6	108–10
10	77	20:7-10	110
		20:11-15	110–12
Revelation	80–82	20:12	110
1:6	109	21:1-4	112
1:12-20	83–85	21:9-27	112–15
1:13	83	21:10	112
2:1-7	85–87	21:19	87
2:1–3:22	84–86	22:1-2	115
2:7	85	22:1-5	115–17
4–5	116	22:2	87
4:1-11	88	22:6-21	116–17
5:6	87	22:19	87
5:6-14	87–90		
5:10	109		
5:13	112		